Karpov *vs.* Korchnoi

World Chess Championship 1978

BENT LARSEN

Introduced by Michael Stean

DAVID McKAY COMPANY, INC.
New York

First American Edition, 1978

ISBN: 0-679-14350-5

LIBRARY OF CONGRESS CATALOG CARD NUMBER: 78-70236

PRINTED IN GREAT BRITAIN

Contents

Explanation of Symbols

0-0	castles king side
0-0-0	castles queen side
!	a strong move
!!	a very strong move
?	a bad move
(?)	a bad move which is not disastrous
??	a blunder
!?	a surprising or interesting move
?!	a dubious move
ch	check
e.p.	en passant

Index of Openings

The numbers refer to pages

BAGUIO?!

Where should the 1978 World Championship match be played? There were seven invitations, seven bids. The four with the highest prize funds, all in the region of one million Swiss Francs, were Hamburg, Graz, Baguio City and Tilburg. The players were asked to set up a list with their order of preference.

Curiously enough Karpov preferred Hamburg, though this was almost home ground for Korchnoi who had been playing for a German club for a short time. Korchnoi preferred Graz, maybe because he was getting used to the Alps - he was living in Switzerland and he felt very well in Evian during the Polugaevsky match.

It seems that at first the small Dutch town of Tilburg sounded good to Karpov, who had won the Interpolis tournament in 1977, but when he enquired and found out that the organizers were not the same as the people who had arranged that tournament, he did not like the idea so much. He knew Hamburg; he had given simultaneous exhibitions and made a T.V. programme there.

If Karpov had put Graz in second place, or Korchnoi Hamburg, the match would have been played in Europe. But both had Baguio as second choice (Karpov actually put Baguio third but left the second spot blank), after which Dr. Euwe gave the match to the Philippines. This was the first title match to be played outside Europe since the famous Capablanca-Alekhine match in Buenos Aires in 1927. Probably many "third world" countries liked this decision. In F.I.D.E. (Fédération Internationale des Echecs - the World Chess Federation) you gain votes by beginning your speech with something like: "F.I.D.E. is not a European organization, it is a world organization!" (In 1939, when the war had started in Europe, the F.I.D.E. congress in Buenos Aires elected an Argentine president, but F.I.D.E.'s founder and president Alexander Rueb simply ignored this election, and the Argentine president is not mentioned in the official books!! When Puerto Rico's Narcisso Rabell Mendez was elected Deputy President in 1970 there was quite a celebration.

Florencio Campomanes, the dynamic leader of Philippine chess during more than two decades, and that country's representative in F.I.D.E. (now Deputy President) thus became the chief organizer of this match. At least as many difficulties were expected as in Reyjkavik 1972 (Fischer-Spassky) and Belgrade 1977 (Spassky-Korchnoi), but Campomanes' many years in national and international chess intrigues have made him a great diplomat, and when charm is called for he can be almost irresistible.

Baguio City is nearly 130 miles north of Manila, at an altitude of about 5,000 feet. It is this altitude which makes the climate relatively pleasant during the hottest part of the year, when those who can afford to do so leave the steaming asphalt jungle of Manila and move into a hotel or a second home in Baguio. Around Easter the city is host to some 80,000 tourists.

Most chess players, like the vast majority of active competitors in all sports, prefer to play their game without being disturbed by political problems. But the choice of Baguio drew some critical comments from people who do not like President Marcos and his government. The match was called a prestige event, like the Muhammad Ali-Joe Frazier boxing match in Manila in 1975. It was considered incredible that a poor country with debts totalling $8,000,000,000 could spend so much money on a chess event ($350,000 to the winner, $200,000 to the loser, plus all the other expenses). It was said that this was an attempt to make Filipinos at home and abroad forget the political problems of their country. For instance, less than 60 miles from Baguio a dam was planned which would flood a vast area of land - land which had been the home of the Bontoc and Kalinga tribes for many centuries. They did not like being moved elsewhere. It is impossible not to feel a certain sympathy for such protests. Yet it is the same problem as occurred in Egypt before the construction of the Aswan dam, and in so many other countries. Changes happen rapidly nowadays, and it is difficult to discover which changes represent progress and which do not. Some people want more electricity, some want to live like their ancestors.

As to the money, the investment probably seemed modest to the Philippine government, which had been ready to spend $5,000,000 on the Fischer-Karpov match which never happened. That was the second biggest purse in sports history, and the largest one that had ever been turned down.

The popularity of chess has grown fantastically in the Philippines during recent years. Asia's first Grandmaster Eugenio Torre is as popular as a film star. Now even Rosendo Balinas has the G.M. title. International tournaments have been organized in the Philippines and a national team was the first to visit China, in 1975. President Marcos declared 1978 "National Chess Year"!

The match was to be held in the brand new convention centre in Baguio. The local chess club, which has 300 members, took part in the preparations. It was not only important for the players, but also for the gentlemen of the press, that good facilities be provided.

Reykjavik 1972 was the first title match outside the Soviet Union in a long time. Baguio 1978 was to be the next one. Memories of Reykjavik haunted the organizers. The West German Grandmaster, arbiter and lawyer Lothar Schmid was appointed chief arbiter, as he had been in Iceland. Experience from Reykjavik was considered important by everyone. Korchnoi wanted to include Lombardy in his team, as Lombardy had been Fischer's official second in Reykjavik and had negotiated with Spassky's representatives. But Lombardy was too expensive!

So Korchnoi continued with the group from Belgrade of Keene, Stean and Murei, who were reinforced, in the middle of the match, by the addition of the Argentine Grandmaster Oscar Panno. Korchnoi's secretary Petra Leeuwerik was called the chief of his delegation by the journalists, as she was often the person who made statements to the press.

On Karpov's side Balashov was the official second. Grandmaster Zaitsev was there too, and of course ex-World Champion Mikhail Tal, although he was listed as a journalist. V. D. Baturinsky represented the Soviet Chess Federation. Korchnoi does not love him, and in his book *Chess is My Life* he

6

calls Baturinsky a petty tyrant, saying that he is "A former prosecutor from the Stalin era, now in honourable retirement". On his way to Manila, when leaving Switzerland, Korchnoi gave a press conference where he read his open letter to Brezhnev in which he asked for permission for his wife and son to leave the Soviet Union. (This letter is given in full on pages 140/141.)

After Korchnoi's arrival in Manila the real diplomatic battle began. The most difficult problem was the flag. Korchnoi wanted to play under the Swiss flag but the Russians stuck to the rules of F.I.D.E. and insisted that F.I.D.E. could not consider Korchnoi to be a representative of Switzerland as he had not yet been a permanent resident there for twelve months. There was no solution. Korchnoi got excited and accused Campomanes and everybody else of favouring the Russians. Campomanes got angry and left the party. Of course this was all ironed out the next day when Edmondson, who could not easily be called pro-Russian, arrived from the U.S.A. He had the solution to the flag problem - no flags at all! Well, no flags on the chess table at least.

This was all very good stuff for the journalists who had already arrived in great numbers. (A special arrangement made it possible to travel from Europe at about half-price.) Korchnoi and his seconds wore little badges with the Swiss flag, but instead of a national anthem Korchnoi had to be satisfied with Beethoven's 9th (Schiller's Ode "To Joy" was originally entitled Ode "To Freedom").

At the opening ceremony the military orchestra made a blunder, playing *The Internationale* instead of the Soviet national anthem. According to some observers it was very bad that Korchnoi remained seated while this was being played. They thought that if President Marcos, whose diplomatic relations with the Russians are still very young, can stand up for the Soviet hymn, everybody should do so. It could also be argued that chess players sit so much that it does them good to stretch their legs now and then.

But in spite of all these difficulties, and in spite of the players' not very friendly feelings towards each other, the match got started. Anything else would have been absurd. Both men wanted to play this match.

BACKGROUND TO THE WORLD CHAMPIONSHIP
by Michael Stean

The World Chess Championship is a triennial event organised under the auspices of F.I.D.E. (Federation International Des Echecs) the world chess federation. However, the modern chess world is turbulent and unpredictable and there has been no World Championship Match for six years. In 1972 Bobby Fischer made the headlines worldwide when he defeated the reigning champion Boris Spassky. Fischer had broken the Soviet monopoly of world chess single-handed and in doing so had captured the interest of many millions of people who had previously had no real involvement in the game. So what has happened to Fischer and the World Championship since then?

Under F.I.D.E. rules Fischer was required to defend his title three years later (1975). His opponent was to be an up and coming young Russian by the name of Karpov, who had unexpectedly brushed aside all opposition (including Spassky!) in a gruelling series of qualifying tournaments and matches to become the official challenger for the title. But of course Fischer as an American and Karpov as a Russian began squabbling over terms and conditions for the forthcoming match. The Soviets negotiated skillfully on Karpov's behalf while Fischer presented his demands rather more bluntly. F.I.D.E. had to arbitrate. They ruled against Fischer with the result that the Russians regained their coveted crown without a single pawn being moved. Thus Anatoly Karpov, a frail, modest-looking young man from Zlatoust (a frail, modest-sounding town in the Urals) had become World Champion, barely twenty four years of age. And Fischer? He has not played a competitive game of chess since defeating Spassky in 1972 and it is difficult to foresee him returning to international or world competition having been stripped of his title away from the chessboard.

To succeed Bobby Fischer, arguably the greatest and unquestionably the most magnetic player of all time, might be considered a pretty daunting prospect, but Karpov proved himself equal to the task. History has shown that world champions rarely compete in many major tournaments during their reigns, but prefer to rest on their laurels until the next World Championship Match is upon them. But not Karpov. Determined to prove himself no mere paper champion he played in major international events with great frequency. His results were phenomenal. He took first place virtually everywhere he played and from his hundreds of games against the world's top players he lost but a handful. The pundits who predicted that Fischer could annihilate Karpov began to swallow their words. The Russians were once more in command of world chess with Karpov at the helm. In the absence of Fischer (still in a state of self-imposed exile from the chessboard), who could possibly hope to topple Karpov?

BACKGROUND TO THE WORLD CHAMPIONSHIP

We must go back to 1974, when Karpov was still battling for the right to challenge for the World Championship. He had just disposed of Spassky with some ease and now had to win one last match. His opponent was Viktor Korchnoi, another Russian. Korchnoi was no newcomer to the chess scene. He had been a leading Grandmaster for some twenty years, but had never quite managed to scale the ultimate heights. At the age of forty three this was considered to be his last chance to try for the World Championship (chessplayers are generally considered to reach their peak in their early thirties and so anybody in excess of forty must be getting "over the hill"). Korchnoi wanted to play in his home city of Leningrad, but the match took place in Moscow over 24 games. After a long and protracted struggle Karpov emerged victorious by the narrowest possible margin 12½-11½.

Korchnoi was not happy about the outcome. He felt that the Soviet authorities had unfairly favoured the younger man. For example, Karpov had a galaxy of stars to help him with his preparation and analysis, whereas Korchnoi experienced great difficulty in finding anybody willing or able to assist him. Certainly the Soviets desperately wanted Karpov to win. Karpov was the rising young star, the hero of the workers, a kind of Proletarian Siegfried, and it was on him that the Russians were pinning their hopes to win back their world title from Fischer.

Korchnoi expressed his sentiments in an interview with a Yugoslav newspaper, but the Soviet authorities did not take kindly to such criticism of Karpov or of themselves. In retaliation they started to take sanctions against Korchnoi. His tournament appearances were suspended and he was not allowed to travel abroad to play. The restrictions were gradually lifted and in the summer of 1976 he was allowed to travel to Amsterdam to play in the I.B.M. international tournament. He never returned. At the end of the tournament instead of reporting to the Soviet Embassy he walked into a police station and asked for political asylum.

So Korchnoi defected. He was denounced by the Soviet Union as a traitor in a letter signed by nearly all the leading Soviet Grandmasters. Curiously enough the signatures of Karpov and Spassky were absent. The Russians also made efforts to expel Korchnoi from the new World Championship cycle, but failed.

Having broken out of the Soviet cocoon, Korchnoi's play found new spirit and fresh vitality at a time in life when it should have been decaying. He stayed in Holland for one year and then moved on to Germany and Switzerland. It was during this period (1977/8) that he gained the right to challenge Karpov in the current World Championship, with victories in matches against Petrosian, Polugaevsky and Spassky. The last three named are all Russian (although Spassky now lives in France) and each of the matches featured a great deal of political "aggro". Petty squabbles, accusations, counter-accusations ranging from spying to hypnotism to "death rays". All very reminiscent of Fischer-Spassky. (During that match the Russians complained that Fischer's chair had been "bugged" to disturb Spassky's concentration. The offending item was taken to pieces, every nut and bolt examined in microscopic detail, and the Soviet claim was substantiated - up to a point. Three dead flies were found)

So the scene is set. Karpov the brilliant young champion. Idol of the Soviet

Union, the man on whom they have pinned all their hopes. Korchnoi the challenger who is "too old". The man who could not tolerate the constraints of Soviet society. The man who defected.

The World Chess Championship 1886-1978

New York, St Louis and New Orleans, January 11 - March 29, 1886
| Steinitz | 1 0 0 0 0 1 1 ½ 1 ½ 1 1 0 ½ ½ 1 ½ 1 1 1 | 12½ |
| Zukertort | 0 1 1 1 1 0 0 ½ 0 ½ 0 0 1 ½ ½ 0 ½ 0 0 0 | 7½ |

Havana, January 20 - February 24, 1889
| Steinitz | 0 1 0 1 1 0 0 1 1 1 0 1 0 1 1 1 ½ | 10½ |
| Chigorn | 1 0 1 0 0 1 1 0 0 0 1 0 1 0 0 0 ½ | 6½ |

New York, December 9, 1980 - January 22, 1891
| Steinitz | ½ 1 ½ 0 0 1 1 ½ ½ 1 ½ 0 1 ½ ½ 0 ½ 1 ½ | 10½ |
| Gunsberg | ½ 0 ½ 1 1 0 0 ½ ½ 0 ½ 1 0 ½ ½ 1 ½ 0 ½ | 8½ |

Havana, January 1 - February 28, 1892
| Steinitz | 0 ½ ½ 1 ½ 1 0 0 ½ 0 1 0 1 1 0 1 0 1 0 1 ½ 1 1 | 12½ |
| Chigorin | 1 ½ ½ 0 ½ 0 1 1 ½ 1 0 1 0 0 1 0 1 0 1 0 ½ 0 0 | 10½ |

New York, Philadelphia and Montreal March 15 - May 26, 1894
| Steinitz | 0 1 0 1 ½ ½ 0 0 0 0 0 ½ 1 1 0 0 1 ½ 0 | 7 |
| Lasker | 1 0 1 0 ½ ½ 1 1 1 1 1 ½ 0 0 1 1 0 ½ 1 | 12 |

Moscow, November 7, 1896 - January 14, 1897
| Lasker | 1 1 1 1 ½ 1 ½ ½ ½ 1 1 0 0 1 ½ 1 1 | 12½ |
| Steinitz | 0 0 0 0 ½ 0 ½ ½ ½ 0 0 1 1 0 ½ 0 0 | 4½ |

New York, Philadelphia, Memphis, Chicago and Baltimore, January 26 - April 6, 1907
| Lasker | 1 1 1 ½ ½ ½ ½ 1 ½ ½ ½ 1 1 1 1 | 11½ |
| Marshall | 0 0 0 ½ ½ ½ ½ 0 ½ ½ ½ 0 0 0 0 | 3½ |

Dusseldorf and Munich, August 17 - September 30, 1908
| Lasker | 1 1 0 1 1 ½ 1 ½ ½ 0 1 0 1 ½ ½ 1 | 10½ |
| Tarasch | 0 0 1 0 0 ½ 0 ½ ½ 1 0 1 0 ½ ½ 0 | 5½ |

Paris, October 19 - November 9, 1909
| Lasker | ½ 1 1 1 1 1 1 ½ 1 1 | 8 |
| Janowski | ½ 0 0 0 0 0 0 ½ 0 0 | 2 |

Vienna and Berlin, January 7 - February 10, 1910
| Lasker | ½ ½ ½ ½ 0 ½ ½ ½ ½ 1 | 5 |
| Schlechter | ½ ½ ½ ½ 1 ½ ½ ½ ½ 0 | 5 |

Berlin, November 8 - December 8, 1910
| Lasker | 1 ½ ½ 1 1 ½ 1 1 1 1 | 9½ |
| Janowski | 0 ½ ½ 0 0 ½ 0 0 0 0 | 1½ |

Havana, March 15 - April 28, 1921

Lasker	½ ½ ½ ½ 0 ½ ½ ½ ½ 0 0 ½ ½ 0	5
Capablanca	½ ½ ½ ½ 1 ½ ½ ½ ½ 1 1 ½ ½ 1	9

Buenos Aires, September 16 - November 29, 1927

Capablanca	0 ½ 1 ½ ½ ½ 1 ½ ½ ½ 0 0 ½ ½ ½ ½ ½ ½ ½ ½ 0 ½ ½ ½ ½ ½ ½ ½ 1 ½ ½ 0 ½ 0	15½
Alekhine	1 ½ 0 ½ ½ ½ 0 ½ ½ ½ 1 1 ½ ½ ½ ½ ½ ½ ½ ½ 1 ½ ½ ½ ½ ½ ½ ½ 0 ½ ½ 1 ½ 1	18½

Germany and Holland, September 6 - November 12, 1929

Alekhine	1 ½ ½ 0 1 0 1 1 ½ 1 ½ 1 0 0 ½ 1 1 0 1 ½ 1 1 ½ ½ ½	15½
Bogoljubow	0 ½ ½ 1 0 1 0 0 ½ 0 ½ 0 1 1 ½ 0 0 1 0 ½ 0 0 ½ ½ ½	9½

Germany, April 1 - June 14, 1934

Alekhine	½ 1 ½ 1 ½ ½ ½ ½ 1 0 1 ½ ½ ½ ½ 1 1 ½ ½ ½ 1 ½ 0 0 1 ½	15½
Bogoljubow	½ 0 ½ 0 ½ ½ ½ ½ 0 1 0 ½ ½ ½ ½ 0 0 ½ ½ ½ 0 ½ 1 1 0 ½	10½

Holland, October 3 - December 15, 1935

Alekhine	1 0 1 1 ½ ½ 1 0 1 0 ½ 0 ½ 0 ½ 1 ½ ½ 1 0 0 ½ ½ ½ 0 0 1 ½ ½ ½	14½
Euwe	0 1 0 0 ½ ½ 0 1 0 1 ½ 1 ½ 1 ½ 0 ½ ½ 0 1 1 ½ ½ ½ 1 1 0 ½ ½ ½	15½

Holland, October 5 - December 16, 1937

Euwe	1 0 ½ ½ 1 0 0 0 ½ 0 ½ ½ 1 0 ½ ½ 1 ½ ½ ½ 0 0 ½ 0 0	9½
Alekhine	0 1 ½ ½ 0 1 1 1 ½ 1 ½ ½ 0 1 ½ ½ 0 ½ ½ ½ 1 1 ½ 1 1	15½

The Hague and Moscow, March 2 - May 17, 1948

		Botvinnik	Smyslov	Keres	Reshevsky	Euwe	
1	Botvinnik	× × × × ×	½ ½ 1 ½ ½	1 1 1 1 0	1 ½ 0 1 1	1 ½ 1 ½ ½	14
2	Smyslov	½ ½ 0 ½ ½	× × × × ×	0 0 ½ 1 ½	½ ½ 1 ½ ½	1 1 0 1 1	11
3	Keres	0 0 0 0 1	1 1 ½ 0 ½	× × × × ×	0 ½ 1 0 ½	1 ½ 1 1 1	10½
4	Reshevsky	0 ½ 1 0 0	½ ½ 0 ½ ½	1 ½ 0 1 ½	× × × × ×	1 ½ ½ 1 1	10½
5	Euwe	0 ½ 0 ½ ½	0 0 1 0 0	0 ½ 0 0 0	0 ½ ½ 0 0	× × × × ×	4

Moscow, March 15 - May 11, 1951

Botvinnik	½ ½ ½ ½ 0 1 1 ½ ½ ½ 0 1 ½ ½ ½ ½ 0 ½ 1 ½ 0 0 1 ½	12
Bronstein	½ ½ ½ ½ 1 0 0 ½ ½ ½ 1 0 ½ ½ ½ ½ 1 ½ 0 ½ 1 1 0 ½	12

Moscow, March 16 - May 13, 1954

Botvinnik	1 1 ½ 1 ½ ½ 0 ½ 0 0 0 1 1 0 1 1 ½ ½ ½ 0 ½ ½ 0 ½	12
Smyslov	0 0 ½ 0 ½ ½ 1 ½ 1 1 1 0 0 1 0 0 ½ ½ ½ 1 ½ ½ 1 ½	12

Moscow, March 5 - April 27, 1957

Botvinnik	0 ½ ½ 1 1 0 ½ 0 ½ ½ ½ 0 1 ½ ½ ½ 0 ½ ½ 0 ½ ½	9½
Smyslov	1 ½ ½ 0 0 1 ½ 1 ½ ½ ½ 1 0 ½ ½ ½ 1 ½ ½ 1 ½ ½	12½

Moscow, March 4 - May 9, 1958

Smyslov	0 0 0 ½ 1 0 ½ ½ ½ ½ 1 0 ½ 0 1 ½ ½ 0 1 ½ ½ 1 ½	10½
Botvinnik	1 1 1 ½ 0 1 ½ ½ ½ ½ 0 1 ½ 1 0 ½ ½ 1 0 ½ ½ 0 ½	12½

Moscow, March 15 - May 7, 1960

Botvinnik	0 ½ ½ ½ ½ 0 0 1 1 ½ 0 ½ ½ ½ ½ ½ 0 ½ 0 ½ ½	8½
Tal	1 ½ ½ ½ ½ 1 1 0 0 ½ 1 ½ ½ ½ ½ ½ 1 ½ 1 ½ ½	12½

Moscow, March 15 - May 12, 1961

Tal	0 1 0 ½ ½ ½ 0 1 0 0 0 1 0 ½ 0 ½ 1 0 1 ½ 0	8
Botvinnik	1 0 1 ½ ½ ½ 1 0 1 1 1 0 1 ½ 1 ½ 0 1 0 ½ 1	13

Moscow, March 23 - May 20, 1963

Botvinnik	1 ½ ½ ½ 0 ½ 0 ½ ½ ½ ½ ½ ½ 1 0 ½ ½ 0 0 ½ ½ ½	9½
Petrosian	0 ½ ½ ½ 1 ½ 1 ½ ½ ½ ½ ½ ½ 0 1 ½ ½ 1 1 ½ ½ ½	12½

Moscow, April 9 - June 9, 1966

Petrosian	½ ½ ½ ½ ½ ½ 1 ½ 1 1 ½ ½ 0 ½ ½ ½ ½ ½ 0 1 ½ 1 0 ½	12½
Spassky	½ ½ ½ ½ ½ ½ 0 ½ ½ 0 ½ ½ 1 ½ ½ ½ ½ ½ 1 0 ½ 0 1 ½	11½

Moscow, April 14 - June 17, 1969

Petrosian	1 ½ ½ 0 0 ½ ½ 0 ½ 1 1 ½ ½ ½ ½ ½ 0 ½ 0 1 0 ½ ½	10½
Spassky	0 ½ ½ 1 1 ½ ½ 1 ½ 0 0 ½ ½ ½ ½ ½ 1 ½ 1 0 1 ½ ½	12½

Reykjavik, July 11 - September 3, 1972

Spassky	1 1 0 ½ 0 0 ½ 0 ½ 0 1 ½ 0 ½ ½ ½ ½ ½ ½ ½ 0	8½
Fischer	0 0 1 ½ 1 1 ½ 1 ½ 1 0 ½ 1 ½ ½ ½ ½ ½ ½ ½ 1	12½

Baguio City, July 16 - October 18, 1978

Karpov	½ ½ ½ ½ ½ ½ ½ 1 ½ ½ 0 ½ 1 1 ½ ½ 1 ½ ½ ½ 0 ½ ½ ½ ½ ½ 1 0 0 ½ 0 1	**6 (16½)**
Korchnoi	½ ½ ½ ½ ½ ½ ½ 0 ½ ½ 1 ½ 0 0 ½ ½ 0 ½ ½ ½ 1 ½ ½ ½ ½ ½ 0 1 1 ½ 1 0	**5 (15½)**

The Roll of Honour

1886-1894	Wilhelm Steinitz
1894-1921	Dr Emanuel Lasker
1921-1927	Jose Raoul Capablanca
1927-1935	Dr Alexander Alekhine
1935-1937	Dr Max Euwe
1937-1946	Dr Alexander Alekhine
1948-1957	Dr Mikhail M. Botvinnik
1957-1958	Vasily Smyslov
1958-1960	Dr Mikhail M. Botvinnik
1960-1961	Mikhail Tal
1961-1963	Dr Mikhail M. Botvinnik
1963-1969	Tigran Petrosian
1969-1972	Boris Spassky
1972-1975	Robert J. Fischer
1975-	Anatoly E. Karpov

THE CHAMPION
by Michael Stean

Anatoly Karpov's rise to the summit of world chess has been meteoric. Born in Zlatoust in the Urals on 23rd May 1951, he learnt to play chess when only four years old. His flair for the game was quickly spotted and he was drawn under the umbrella of a Soviet system that develops outstanding talent for chess from a very early age. (By the age of 12 he was already receiving tuition from ex-World Champion Mikhail Botvinnik). His first trip to the West came in 1967 when he represented the U.S.S.R. in the European Junior Championship in Groningen, Holland. He won in a canter. Two years later he won the World Junior Championship in Stockholm with equal ease.

The transition from junior chess to senior chess is a difficult one. To win the World Junior Championship requires great talent, but the test of genius is whether one can progress to challenge the great masters of the game who have been studying chess all their life. At the end of 1971 Karpov competed in the Alekhine Memorial Tournament in Moscow, one of the toughest events in the world, containing a host of great names. He shared first place with Leonid Stein (ahead of Korchnoi inter alia) and so had already established himself as a major force in world chess, though still only twenty years old.

Success followed success and by sharing first place in the powerful Interzonal tournament in Leningrad in 1973 Karpov qualified at the first attempt for the final stages of the World Championship cycle, the Candidates' Matches. (The eight qualifiers for the Candidates' stage play matches on a knock-out system to decide the official challenger for the World Championship). It was widely believed at the time that Karpov was still too young to succeed at this level. After all, it was still just a few years since he had graduated from the ranks of junior competition and here he was face to face with the established giants of the chess world. Still, no doubt the experience would stand him in good stead for the next cycle. Karpov had other ideas. In the first round he beat Polugaevsky without conceding a single game and in the semi-final he totally out-classed Spassky. Admittedly Spassky was below his best in that match, but it was the youthful Karpov who was displaying the greater authority and maturity of play against the veritable ex-World Champion. The final match saw the long, controversial and sometimes bitter struggle against Korchnoi already mentioned. So Karpov became the World Championship challenger at the end of 1974 and in Fischer's absence assumed the title of World Champion a few months later.

To pick Karpov out of a crowd would not be easy. Slight in build, mild in manner he appears very much to typify the lad who lives next door. As such his widespread popularity within the Soviet Union is not difficult to understand. He looks like one of the masses and so the masses find it easy to identify with him. But his modest exterior belies his iron will to win, his fierce ambition, his total self-assurance. Though polite and unassuming across a dinner table, across the chessboard he becomes hard, almost ruthless and quite merciless. His play is scientific, but highly practical. He rarely allows himself to be sidetracked from the central theme or worried by diversionary tactics. Karpov has no clearly defined or definable style but the single most characterising facet of his play is his avoidance of risk. Not that he is afraid. Karpov has an excellent temperament and nerves of steel, but he nevertheless prefers always to be in complete control of the situation. He moves very quickly, reminiscent of Fischer, and will often rush or "blitz" his opponent near the time control. It is in these last few minutes when the opponent is pressed for time that Karpov is so merciless. His speed of thought is exceptional and he has the ability to "create trouble", continuously probing, manoevring, regrouping, while playing his moves almost instantaneously, so that his poor opponent, pressed for time, is given no respite between moves and is worried, almost bullied into making mistakes. And always of course Karpov is in control. No risk, nothing left to chance. This explains why he is so hard to beat. Karpov will generally lose less games in a year than most players lose in a single tournament! Cool, clinical and precise, Karpov is a formidable opponent.

Has Karpov any weaknesses? If he does they are certainly not easy to discern, but the one thing that may count against him is ironically the very fact that he is so successful. Karpov has never experienced a major setback in his career. He may some time have been dissatisfied with one or two of his results, but disaster has never stared him in the face. However, losing this match would be a disaster for the Soviet Union and, *per se*, for Karpov. Spassky went through a very difficult period in Russia after losing to Fischer in 1972 and Karpov has no reason to suppose he will escape a similar backlash if he falls victim to Korchnoi this time. So if and when there occurs a crisis point during the match how will Karpov react? He is well renowned for his coolness under pressure, but he is now in a new situation. In the last World Championship cycle he was playing the rôle of the young hopeful aspiring to the great heights, and honourable defeat would have been acceptable, close defeat even creditable. Now he is Champion playing against the declared enemy of the U.S.S.R. and defeat cannot be contemplated. It is not an easy burden to bear.

Technically, however, Karpov is almost flawless. His opening play is strong and backed by very thorough and diligent preparation. Karpov did not become a great player by the grace of God alone. He works very hard and has over recent years developed a wide and thorough knowledge of opening theory. His middlegame play is fluent and sound, and, once he has developed a concrete plan of action, remorselessly accurate. He has a particular talent of reducing a complex overall strategy to a series of seemingly simple and effortless moves.

His endgame play is a similar combination of effortlessness and precision. Comparisons with Fischer and Capablanca come naturally, but Karpov is more practically orientated, more pragmatic. To Karpov chess is a fight, and a fight he is accustomed to winning.

THE CHALLENGER
by Michael Stean

Born in Leningrad, 23 July 1931, Viktor Korchnoi is one of the most experienced and long-standing Grandmasters currently active in world chess. Unlike Karpov he was no childhood genius or overnight success. Competition for the top honours in Soviet chess is strong and Korchnoi had to battle long and hard to establish himself. His first international tournament did not come until 1954 in Bucharest (which he won) by which time he was of course twenty three, an age at which Karpov was already virtually World Champion. Nor was his ascent smooth and untroubled. Disappointments mingled with the successes and it was not until the 1960s that he truly established himself as a major force in world chess. Korchnoi is renowned worldwide for his almost superhuman determination and will to win, and it was probably during these difficult early years that he developed such gritty fighting qualities. Chess can be a cruel game, especially when as a professional in Eastern Europe your livelihood depends on your success at the board.

Despite his occasional setbacks Korchnoi has amassed a vast, almost unrivalled string of tournament victories stretching back over a period of nearly a quarter of a century. Some of these wins are quite startling in dimension; for example Gyula 1965 where he scored 14½ out of 15, or Beverwijk 1968 where he won by a margin of three clear points ahead of players such as Tal, Portisch, Hort ..... Nevertheless this is Korchnoi's first World Championship Match. He has already come close to a shot at the World Title three times, but three times he has stumbled when in sight of his goal. In 1962 when the Candidates' stage (the final elimination stage) was played as a tournament as opposed to the present day knock-out series of matches, he finished 5th in the Candidates' Tournament but did have the distinction of beating Fischer. In 1968 he reached the final of the Candidates' (which was by now a knock-out) only to lose to Spassky. His third near miss has already been referred to, the narrow and hotly-disputed loss to Karpov in Moscow 1974. Little did he know at the time that Fischer would not defend his title and that by winning that match he would be the present-day World Champion instead of Karpov.

Falling as he did at the last hurdle in 1974 might have dampened the spirit of lesser men, especially at the age of forty three, but Korchnoi, now a free man in the West, summoned his apparently endless reserves for a fourth attempt. And as if fate had been written by a Hollywood script-writer, he succeeded. Narrow victory in a bitterly fought quarter-final against Petrosian was followed by a crushing win over Polugaevsky. Once more into a final against Spassky, his old friend and rival. A bitter and controversial struggle ensued. The fight was not confined to the chessboard and the match turned sour. Despite losing four games in succession at one point, Korchnoi won 10½-7½ and so had at last realised his great ambition, a match for the world title.

It is quite incredible that now, at the age of forty seven, after nearly thirty years as a chessplayer, Korchnoi is playing better than at any time in his life. His current strength can only be attributed to his monumental willpower and determination to succeed. But his source of strength is also his source of weakness. His determination as a player insists that he plays every game to win - at all costs. Not for him the careful safety-first precision of Karpov. Korchnoi is the insurance man's nightmare. Always running risks, always trying to complicate, always rocking the boat, heedless of who it is that might fall out. His restless, impatient, sometimes impetuous play often brought him to the brink of disaster. Middle age has added a touch of stability to his play, maybe this was the vital missing ingredient that has brought him to the top, but the old horse is still always straining at the bit, fighting for his head. A shameless and tireless battler, Korchnoi will never go down for want of trying.

Stylistically, Korchnoi insists his play is entirely classical, but his games generally lack the fluency or harmony of Fischer or Capablanca. Instead Korchnoi injects his own very special brand of drama into the game. Strategically he is very deep, but such depth of play requires considerable thought. He also calculates many moves ahead, probably more so than any of his contemporaries, but this also consumes time. As a result he often runs himself desperately short of time on the clock. Hair-raising time-scrambles ensue with moves crashing down faster than the eye can follqw. Naturally anything can happen in such situations and his games are often won or lost in those last few frantic seconds. But whatever the position on the board, whatever the time on the clock, you can be sure Korchnoi is trying his utmost to complicate, and you can be sure he is trying to win. The word draw has no meaning to him. If Karpov can be said to make the pieces dance, then Korchnoi makes them tremble with fear!

Perhaps the only way to describe Korchnoi's style is as classical, but highly individual. He certainly adheres to all the generally accepted principles of chess theory, almost passionately so, but he has his own interpretations and this is the only way he can play.

Korchnoi cannot easily accede to dogma and probably this is the root of his split with the Soviet Union. He never shies away from confrontation over the chessboard, but his audacity in challenging establishment figures within the U.S.S.R. led him into deep trouble there and eventually forced him to defect. Since the break his play has blossomed, but has lost none of its eccentric brilliance. His last two tournaments prior to this match were in Wijk aan Zee (Holland), where he finished second in a strong field (after losing to the player who came last!), and Beersheva (Israel) where he won with a score of 12/13, no less than four points ahead of the second placed player!

So this sums up Korchnoi - brilliant, with vast experience, but erratic. At the height of his form he is completely unstoppable, but can he realise his full potential when it counts, and for how long?

PREVIOUS ENCOUNTERS

Before the present match Karpov and Korchnoi had met 36 times. Karpov had won seven, Korchnoi six and twenty three had been drawn.

White: Korchnoi
Black: Karpov

Simultaneous Display
Cheliabinsk 1962

Scotch Four Knights

1 P-K4 P-K4 2 N-KB3 N-QB3 3 P-Q4 PxP 4 NxP N-B3 5 N-QB3 P-Q3 6 B-QN5 B-Q2 7 0-0 B-K2 8 R-K1 0-0 9 B-B1 R-K1 10 P-KR3 NxN 11 QxN B-B3 12 B-K3 Q-Q2 13 QR-Q1 B-B1 14 B-KN5 B-K2 15 B-B1 P-QR3 16 P-KN4 P-R3 17 P-B4 QR-Q1 18 B-N2 Q-B1 19 Q-Q3 P-QN4 20 P-R3 Q-N2 21 Q-B3 B-B1 22 P-KR4 P-QR4 23 P-N5 PxP 24 RPxP N-R2 25 B-R3 P-Q4 26 PxP RxRch 27 RxR BxQP 28 NxB QxN 29 QxQ RxQ 30 P-N6 B-B4ch Draw agreed.

White: Korchnoi
Black: Karpov

38th USSR Championship
Riga 1970

English Opening

1 P-QB4 P-QB4 2 N-KB3 N-KB3 3 N-B3 P-Q4 4 PxP NxP 5 P-Q4 PxP 6 QxP NxN 7 QxN N-B3 8 P-K4 P-QR3 9 B-QB4 Q-R4 10 B-Q2 QxQ 11 BxQ P-K3 12 0-0 R-KN1 13 KR-Q1 P-QN4 14 B-Q3 P-B3 15 P-QR4 P-N5 16 B-Q4 NxB 17 NxN B-B4 18 B-B4 BxN 19 RxB K-K2 20 QR-Q1 R-R2 21 P-QN3 P-QR4 22

R-Q6 B-Q2 23 P-B4 R-QB1 24 P-K5 PxP 25 PxP R-B4 26 R-K1 P-R3 27 P-R4 R-R1 28 R-K3 R-B3 29 R-Q4 R-B4 30 R-Q6 R-B3 31 RxR BxR 32 R-N3 R-KN1 33 K-B2 P-N4 34 K-K3 P-N5 35 K-Q4 P-R4 36 K-B5 B-K5 37 K-N6 R-QR1 38 B-Q3 B-B4 39 R-K3 R-QB1 40 B-B4 B-B7 41 K-N5 R-QR1 42 R-K2 B-N3 43 P-N3 B-B4 44 R-Q2 B-K5 45 R-Q6 B-Q4 46 BxB PxB 47 RxP K-K3 48 R-B5 R-R2 49 K-N6 R-Q2 50 KxP R-Q6 51 KxP RxKNP 52 P-R5 R-N8 53 R-B2 P-N6 54 R-QR2 R-KR8 55 P-R6 RxPch 56 K-B3 R-R6 57 R-KN2 Black resigns.

White: Karpov
Black: Korchnoi

Training Match
Leningrad 1971
1st Match Game

Ruy Lopez

1 P-K4 P-K4 2 N-KB3 N-QB3 3 B-N5 P-QR3 4 B-R4 N-B3 5 0-0 B-K2 6 R-K1 P-QN4 7 B-N3 P-Q3 8 P-B3 0-0 9 P-KR3 N-N1 10 P-Q4 QN-Q2 11 QN-Q2 B-N2 12 B-B2 R-K1 13 N-B1 B-KB1 14 N-N3 P-N3 15 B-N5 P-R3 16 B-Q2 B-N2 17 P-QR4 N-N3 18 RPxP RPxP 19 P-N3 N(B3)-Q2 20 B-Q3 P-N5 21 RxR BxR 22 QPxP NxP(K4) 23 NxN PxN 24 Q-B2 PxP 25 BxBP Q-Q3 26 N-B1 R-Q1 27 B-K2 Q-B4 28 N-Q2 Q-B3 29 B-B1 B-N2 30 Q-N2 B-QB1 31 N-B3 P-B3 32 N-Q2 B-K3 33 R-B1 Q-B4 34 N-B3 Q-Q3 35 B-R5 B-KB1 36 Q-B3 P-QB4

17

37 B-B4 R-N1 38 BxN QxB 39 N-R4 K-R2 40 R-Q1 BxB 41 PxB R-Q1 42 R-R1 Q-N2 43 Q-B3 B-N2 44 R-R5 R-Q5 45 RxP Q-N8ch 46 K-R2 QxP 47 QxQ RxQ 48 P-N4 P-R4 49 K-N3 PxP 50 PxP R-Q5 51 R-B7 R-Q6ch 52 P-B3 P-K5 53 R-K7 PxP 54 NxBP R-B6 55 R-QB7 K-N1 Draw agreed.

White: Karpov
Black: Korchnoi

Training Match
Leningrad 1971
2nd Match Game

Ruy Lopez

1 P-K4 P-K4 2 N-KB3 N-QB3 3 B-N5 P-QR3 4 B-R4 N-B3 5 0-0 NxP 6 P-Q4 P-QN4 7 B-N3 P-Q4 8 PxP B-K3 9 P-B3 B-K2 10 QN-Q2 Q-Q2 11 R-K1 N-B4 12 B-B2 P-Q5 13 N-K4 PxP 14 PxP 0-0-0 15 Q-K2 B-B5 16 NxN BxN 17 Q-K4 K-N2 18 B-K3 B-Q4 19 Q-KB4 B-R6 20 QR-Q1 P-R3

21 RxB QxR 22 B-K4 Q-B5 23 N-Q4 QxBP 24 BxNch K-N1 25 R-KB1 RxN 26 BxR QxB(3) 27 QxBP R-Q1 28 B-K3 Q-Q4 29 P-K6 R-KB1 30 QxNP R-K1 31 B-B4 Q-B5 32 Q-N3 B-N7 33 R-K1 B-B6 34 Q-N6 R-K2 35 R-K4 QxRP 36 P-KR4 B-Q5 37 B-N3

P-N5 38 K-R2 Q-Q4 39 Q-N4 B-B4 40 RxPch K-R2 Black resigns.

White: Karpov
Black: Korchnoi

Training Match
Leningrad 1971
3rd Match Game

French Defence

Notes by Korchnoi

1	P-K4	P-K3
2	P-Q4	P-Q4
3	N-Q2	P-QB4
4	KN-B3	N-QB3
5	KPxP	KPxP
6	B-N5	B-Q3
7	PxP	Q-K2ch?!

Better is 7...BxBP 8 0-0 N-K2.

8 Q-K2!

Also good for White is 8 B-K2 BxBP 9 N-N3 but the text is more accurate.

8 ... BxBP

Against Tal in the 1973 USSR Championship I exchanged queens in this position.

9	N-N3	B-N3
10	N-K5!	K-B1!?

Also possible is 10...B-Q2 11 NxB KxN when 12 B-KB4 keeps White's advantage.

11 B-KB4

If 11 NxN PxN 12 BxP QxQch (not 12...BxPch?? 13 K-Q1! winning at least a piece) 13 KxQ B-R3ch with compensation for the pawn.

11	...	Q-B3
12	B-N3	P-KR4
13	P-KR4	KN-K2
14	0-0-0	NxN?!

Better is 14...B-K3 followed by ...R-K1 and ...N-B4.

| 15 | BxN | QxBP |

16	BxPch	KxB
17	QxN	B-KB4
18	Q-K5ch!	

If 18 B-Q3 Q-K6ch 19 QxQ BxQch 20 K-N1 B-N5 with equal chances.

18	...	P-B3
19	Q-K7ch	K-N3
20	R-Q2!!	

If 20 B-Q3 BxB 21 RxB QR-QB1 22 P-B3 KR-K1 with roughly equal chances. Also playable is 20...QR-QB1.

20	...	B-K6
21	R-B1	BxRch
22	NxB	Q-Q5!

Not 22...QxRP 23 RxB KxR 24 B-Q3ch K-B5 25 Q-N4ch winning nor 22...QxNP 23 RxB KxR 24 B-Q3ch K-B5 25 QxBPch winning.

23	RxB!	KxR
24	B-Q3ch	K-B5
25	Q-Q6ch	Q-K4
26	Q-N4ch	P-Q5?!

After 26...K-N6 27 N-B1ch KxP 28 Q-Q2ch K-R6 29 B-B5ch (or 29 Q-B2 KR-KN1 30 B-B5ch R-N5) 29...KxP the position is unclear.

| 27 | N-K4! | K-B4? |

27...K-N5 was better. Now White wins by force.

28	QxNP	K-N5
29	B-K2ch	KxP
30	P-N3ch	K-R6
31	N-B2ch	K-R7

Or 31...KxP 32 Q-B3ch K-R5 33 N-K4 followed by 34 Q-R1ch.

32	Q-R1ch	KxP
33	N-K4ch	K-B5
34	Q-B3 mate	

One of the best games he has played in his whole life.

White: Karpov
Black: Korchnoi

Training Match
Leningrad 1971
4th Match Game

Sicilian Defence

1 P-K4 P-QB4 2 N-KB3 P-K3 3 P-Q4 PxP 4 NxP N-KB3 5 N-QB3 P-Q3 6 B-K2 B-K2 7 B-K3 P-QR3 8 P-B4 Q-B2 9 P-KN4 P-Q4 10 P-K5 N-K5 11 NxN PxN 12 P-KR4 0-0 13 P-N5 R-Q1

19

14 P-B3 N-B3 15 Q-Q2 B-B4 16 P-R̃5 B-Q2 17 B-N4 B-K1 18 P-N6 Q-R4 19 PxBPch BxP 20 NxN PxN 21 Q-KB2 BxB 22 QxB QR-N1 23 P-N4 Q-R6 24 Q-B1 Q-R5 25 B-K2 P-B4 26 PxP Q-B3 27 Q-K3 R-N7 28 KR-N1 BxP 29 B-B4 Q-R5 30 BxPch K-R1 31 B-N4 BxB 32 RxB RxP White resigns.

White: Korchnoi
Black: Karpov

Training Match
Leningrad 1971
5th Match Game

Queen's Indian Defence

1 P-Q4 N-KB3 2 P-QB4 P-K3 3 N-KB3 P-QN3 4 P-KN3 B-N2 5 B-N2 B-K2 6 0-0 0-0 7 P-Q5 PxP 8 N-Q4 N-B3 9 PxP NxN 10 QxN P-B4 11 Q-Q2 P-Q3 12 N-B3 P-QR3 13 P-N3 N-Q2 14 P-QR4 R-N1 15 R-N1 B-B1 16 R-Q1 R-K1 17 B-QR3 Q-B2 18 P-QN4 N-K4 19 Q-B4 B-Q2 20 P-R3 R(K1)-QB1 21 P-N5 R-R1 22 B-QB1 PxP 23 PxP R-R4 24 Q-K4 B-KB3 25 Q-B2 R(B1)-R1 26 K-R1 N-N3 27 B-N2 Q-Q1 28 P-B4 Q-K1 29 P-K4 BxNP 30 NxB RxN 31 BxB PxB 32 RxR QxR 33 R-QN1 Q-R3 34 P-R4 K-N2 35 P-R5 N-B1 36 Q-Q1 P-R3 37 Q-N4ch K-R1 38 Q-B5 N-R2 39 P-K5

QPxP 40 P-Q6 Q-K7 41 P-Q7 K-N2 42 RxP R-R7 43 Q-R3 R-Q7 44 R-N2 RxR 45 P-Q8 = Q N-B1 46 PxP PxP 47 Q(8)-R4 R-N5 48 P-KN4 R-KB5 49 Q(R4)-N3 N-K3 50 Q-K3 Draw agreed.

White: Karpov
Black: Korchnoi

Training Match
Leningrad 1971
6th Match Game

Sicilian Defence

1 P-K4 P-QB4 2 N-KB3 P-Q3 3 P-Q4 PxP 4 NxP N-KB3 5 N-QB3 P-KN3 6 B-K3 B-N2 7 P-B3 N-B3 8 B-QB4 0-0 9 Q-Q2 B-Q2 10 B-N3 R-B1 11 0-0-0 N-K4 12 B-R6 N-N5 13 BxN BxB 14 QxB RxB 15 P-KR4 Q-R4 16 N-N3 Q-K4 17 N-Q5 KR-B1 18 P-B3 B-B3 19 NxNch QxN 20 K-N1 P-Q4 21 PxP Q-B4ch 22 K-R1 BxP 23 P-R5 P-K3 24 N-Q4 Q-B3 25 PxP RPxP 26 P-KN4 Q-N2 27 Q-K3 R(5)-B4 28 R-R2 P-QN4 29 N-N3 R-B5 30 R-Q4 RxR 31 NxR P-N5 32 P-KB4 P-R4 33 N-N5 Q-B3 34 P-N5 Q-N2 35 K-N1 P-B3 36 N-Q6 R-Q1 37 N-K4 BPxP 38 KBPxP BxNch 39 QxB Q-KB2

40 R-K2 Q-B8ch 41 R-K1 R-Q8ch 42

K-B2 RxR 43 QxNPch K-B1 White resigns.

White: Korchnoi
Black: Karpov

Moscow 1971

English Opening

1 P-QB4 P-QB4 2 N-KB3 N-KB3 3 P-KN3 P-Q4 4 PxP NxP 5 B-N2 P-KN3 6 P-Q4 B-N2 7 P-K4 N-B2 8 P-Q5 N-N4 9 0-0-0 10 Q-B2 N-R3 11 B-B4 B-N5 12 QN-Q2 N-Q5 13 NxN PxN 14 N-B3 Q-N3 15 N-K5 BxN 16 BxB P-B3 17 B-B4 QR-B1 18 Q-R4 P-N4 19 B-B1 B-K7 20 R-K1 P-Q6 21 B-B1 BxB 22 RxB R-B7 23 B-K3 N-B4 24 Q-Q4 P-K4 25 PxPe.p. QxKP 26 QR-B1 R-B1 27 P-QN4 NxP

28 RxR PxR 29 R-B1 P-N3 30 P-B3 N-Q3 31 Q-Q3 R-B3 32 P-QR4 Q-B5 33 Q-Q2 N-B2 34 P-B4 P-N5 35 P-N5 R-B1 36 Q-Q7 P-KR4 37 K-B2 Q-B6 38 Q-B5 R-K1 White resigns.

White: Korchnoi
Black: Karpov

Hastings 1971-72

Queen's Pawn Opening

Notes by Korchnoi

1	P-Q4	N-KB3
2	N-KB3	P-K3
3	B-N5	P-QN3

3...P-QB4 is normal.

4	P-K4	P-KR3
5	BxN	QxB
6	B-Q3	B-N2
7	QN-Q2	P-Q3
8	Q-K2	P-R3

I was rather expecting 8...Q-Q1 followed by ...B-K2 and ...0-0. It is natural for such an undeveloping move as 8...Q-Q1 to go against the grain, but I felt that the queen was misplaced on B3 and expected Karpov to retreat her at more than one stage. The course of the game repeatedly reinforced my opinion.

9	0-0-0	N-Q2
10	K-N1	P-K4

10...Q-Q1 11 N-B4.

11	P-B3	B-K2

I had still been expecting 11...Q-Q1!

12	N-B4	0-0
13	B-B2	KR-K1

Perhaps 13...PxP should have been played first, even though it appears dangerously to strengthen White's centre; the point being that after 14 PxP KR-K1 would have some counter-attacking effect. However 15 P-K5 would still leave White on top.

14	P-Q5!	P-B4

After long thought, but a bad move. 14...P-B3 seems indicated.

15	N-K3

Now White is all set to start a direct attack by 16 P-KN4.

15	...	B-KB1
16	P-KN4	Q-Q1
17	P-N5	P-KR4

If 17...PxP then 18 QR-N1.

18	P-N6!	PxP
19	KR-N1	Q-B3
20	N-N5	B-K2
21	N-K6	N-B1

After the game I asked Karpov whether he had overlooked the loss of the exchange. "No", he replied, "I invited it, feeling that in view of the strength of your advanced knight, it was my best chance". But 21...QR-B1 seemed to me a natural measure, e.g. 22 R-N2 N-B1 23 QR-N1 K-R2 24 NxNch RxN 25 RxP QxR 26 RxQ KxR 27 N-B5; White has B-Q1, P-KB4 etc. to follow with probably a winning attack, but the game is not over by any means. After the text move Black really has little or no prospect of salvation.

22	N-B7	Q-B2
23	QR-KB1?	

With victory in sight I begin to relax. I have the K-side under control and should now have killed Black's prospects on the Q-side as well. I am convinced that the one correct move here was 23 P-QR4 followed by P-N3, B-Q3, K-B2 etc.

23	...	P-QN4?

Inaccurate play on both sides. 23...QR-B1 24 NxR QxN would have cost me a clear tempo.

24	NxQR?!	BxN?

It would have been easier to bring the rook back into the game, after 24...RxN, than to reactivate this very poor bishop.

25	P-QB4	R-N1
26	B-Q3	Q-K1?

Black should have reconciled himself to 26...P-N5.

27	R-B1	B-KB3
28	R-N2	R-N3?

So as to play 29...B-N2 and 30...B-B1 but I am able to ensure that he never has time. Still better is 28...P-N5.

29	QR-N1	R-N1

Forced because White threatened 30 RxP NxR 31 QxP.

30	Q-B1	P-N5

After 30...B-N2 31 PxP B-B1 32 PxP B-R6 33 Q-K2 BxR 34 RxB White should win.

32 B-K2!

Again threatening 32 RxP, and this time there is no defence.

31	...	P-R5
32	RxP	QxR

Or 32...NxR 33 B-R5 winning.

33	RxQ	NxR
34	B-N4	N-B5
35	Q-Q1	P-N6

Agony!

36	PxP	B-N2
37	N-N2	B-B1

If 37...NxN then, of course, 38 B-K6ch K-B1 39 Q-R5.

38	BxB	RxB
39	Q-N4	R-K1
40	NxN	PxN
41	QxBP	B-K4
42	QxP	R-KB1
43	P-N4	B-Q5
44	PxP	Resigns

White: Karpov
Black: Korchnoi

Leningrad 1973
Interzonal Tournament

Pirc Defence

1 P-K4 P-Q3 2 P-Q4 N-KB3 3 N-QB3 P-KN3 4 N-B3 B-N2 5 B-K2 0-0 6 0-0 N-B3 7 P-Q5 N-N1 8 P-KR3 P-B3 9 P-QR4 P-QR4 10 B-KN5 B-Q2 11 R-R-K1 N-R3 12 PxP BxBP 13 B-N5

N-QN5 14 Q-K2 P-R3 15 B-KB4 P-K4 16 B-R2 R-B1 17 QR-Q1 Q-K2 18 R-Q2 P-R4 Draw agreed.

White: Korchnoi
Black: Karpov

41st USSR Championship
Moscow 1973

Polish Defence

1 N-KB3 N-KB3 2 P-KN3 P-QN4 3 P-B3 B-N2 4 P-QR4 P-QR3 5 P-K3 N-B3 6 P-Q4 P-K3 7 P-QN4 B-K2 8 QN-Q2 N-R2 9 B-Q3 0-0 10 P-K4 P-Q3 11 0-0 P-B4 12 NPxP QPxP 13 B-N2 N-B3 14 P-K5 N-Q4 15 PxNP PxNP 16 Q-N1 PxP 17 PxP P-R3 18 BxP Q-N3 19 B-K2 RxR 20 BxR Q-R2 21 N-B4 R-N1 22 B-N2 R-R3 23 Q-B2 Q-N2 24 B-R1 N(3)-N5 25 Q-Q2 R-QB1 26 N-K3 NxN 27 QxN(K3) BxB 28 QxB R-B7 29 Q-Q1 Q-B3 30 P-R3 N-Q4 31 Q-Q3 Q-R5 32 N-Q2 R-R7 33 N-N3 N-N5 34 Q-N1 N-Q4 35 R-B1 Q-R1 36 R-B8ch QxR 37 QxR Q-B5 38 Q-N1 Q-K7 39 Q-QB1 B-N4 40 Q-B1 Q-B6 41 P-R4

White resigns.

Moscow, 16 September - 22 November, 1974

	1	2	3	4	5	6	7	8	9	0	1	2	3	4	5	6	7	8	9	0	1	2	3	4	
Karpov	½	1	½	½	½	1	½	½	½	½	½	½	½	½	½	½	1	½	0	½	0	½	½	½	12½
Korchnoi	½	0	½	½	½	0	½	½	½	½	½	½	½	½	½	½	0	½	1	½	1	½	½	½	11½

White: Korchnoi
Black: Karpov

Moscow 1974
Final Candidates Match
1st Match Game

English Opening

1 P-QB4 N-KB3 2 N-QB3 P-K3 3 N-B3 P-QN3 4 P-K4 B-N2 5 Q-K2 B-N5 6 P-K5 N-N1 7 P-Q4 P-Q3 8 B-Q2 PxP 9 PxP N-QR3 10 0-0-0 Q-K2 11 P-KN3 0-0-0 12 B-N2 N-B4 13 B-N5 P-KB3 14 RxRch QxR 15 R-Q1 Q-K1 16 PxP PxP 17 B-Q2 N-K2 18 N-K4 NxN 19 BxB N-B3 20 B-R3 P-B4 21 N-K1 Q-N3 22 P-B3 N-N4 23 P-B4 N-K5 24 N-B3 Q-B3 25 Q-K3 R-Q1 26 RxRch NxR 27 N-N5 Q-N3 28 N-B3 Q-B3 29 B-N4 P-B4 30 B-K1 N-B2 31 B-B1 B-B3 32 B-Q3 K-N2 33 P-KR3 Q-R3 34 P-KR4 Q-N3 35 N-N5 N(2)-Q3 36 N-B3 N-B2 37 N-N5 N(2)-B3 Draw agreed.

White: Karpov
Black: Korchnoi

Moscow 1974
Final Candidates Match
2nd Match Game

Sicilian Defence

1 P-K4 P-QB4 2 N-KB3 P-Q3 3 P-Q4 PxP 4 NxP N-KB3 5 N-QB3 P-KN3 6 B-K3 B-N2 7 P-B3 N-B3 8 Q-Q2 0-0 9 B-QB4 B-Q2 10 P-KR4 R-B1 11 B-N3 N-K4 12 0-0-0 N-B5 13 BxN RxB 14 P-R5 NxRP 15 P-KN4 N-B3 16 N(4)-K2 Q-R4 17 B-R6 BxB 18 QxB KR-B1 19 R-Q3 R(5)-B4

20 P-N5 RxP 21 R-Q5 RxR 22 NxR R-K1 23 N(2)-B4 B-B3 24 P-K5 BxN 25 PxN PxP 26 QxRPch K-B1 27 Q-R8ch Black resigns.

White: Korchnoi
Black: Karpov

Moscow 1974
Final Candidates Match
3rd Match Game

English Opening

1 P-QB4 N-KB3 2 N-QB3 P-K3 3 N-B3 P-QN3 4 P-K4 B-N2 5 Q-K2 B-N5 6 P-K5 N-N1 7 P-Q4 N-K2 8 B-Q2 0-0 9 0-0-0 P-Q4 10 P-KR4 BxN 11 BxB PxP 12 QxP B-R3 13 Q-R4 BxB 14 KRxB Q-Q4 15 K-N1 P-QR4

16 Q-B2 P-R3 17 KR-K1 N-R3 18
Q-K4 KR-Q1 19 QxQ RxQ 20 R-Q2
QR-Q1 21 KR-Q1 P-R4 22 K-B2
N-KB4 23 P-KN3 P-KB3 24 PxP PxP
25 N-N1 N-K2 26 N-K2 N-N3 27
R-Q3 N-N5ch 28 BxN PxB 29 P-R3
PxP 30 RxP R(1)-Q2 31 R-K1 K-B2
32 R-Q3 R-KB4 33 P-B3 P-B4 34
P-B4 N-K2 35 PxP RxQBPch 36
N-B3 R(2)-B2 37 K-Q2 N-B4 38
R-QR1 R-B5 39 R-R6 P-N4 40 P-N3
R-N5 41 N-K2 K-K2 42 R-R8 R-Q2 43
RxRch KxR 44 R-R8 RxNP 45 RxP
NxNP 46 NxN RxN 47 RxP P-B4 48
K-K2 R-N5 49 K-B3 RxRP 50 R-N6
R-R8 51 R-R6 R-QB8 52 K-N3 R-B5
53 K-B3 R-B6ch 54 K-B2 R-B3 55
R-R1 R-B5 56 K-B3 K-Q3 57 R-K1
R-B6ch Draw agreed.

White: Karpov
Black: Korchnoi

Moscow 1974
Final Candidates Match
4th Match Game

French Defence

1 P-K4 P-K3 2 P-Q4 P-Q4 3 N-Q2
P-QB4 4 KPxP KPxP 5 KN-B3
N-QB3 6 B-N5 B-Q3 7 PxP BxBP 8
0-0 N-K2 9 N-N3 B-Q3 10 P-B3
B-KN5 11 N(N3)-Q4 0-0 12 B-K2
R-K1 13 R-K1 P-QR3 14 B-KN5
P-R3 15 B-R4 Q-N3 16 Q-N3 B-QB4
17 QxQ BxQ 18 B-Q3 K-B1 19 P-QR3
NxN 20 NxN BxN 21 PxB N-B4 22
P-B3 NxB 23 PxB N-N3 24 P-KN3
N-K2 25 B-B1 N-B3 26 B-N2 RxRch
27 RxR R-Q1 28 K-B2 R-Q3 29 R-Q1
K-K2 30 P-N4 R-Q1 31 K-K3 K-Q3 32
R-KB1 P-B3 33 R-B1 R-QB1 34 R-B5
N-K2 35 B-B1 R-K1 36 K-Q2 P-B4 37
B-K2 PxP 38 BxNP R-KB1 39 R-B2
P-KN3 40 K-K3 P-KR4 41 B-R3 N-B3
42 R-Q2 P-QN4 43 B-N2 P-R4 44
P-KR4 PxP 45 PxP R-K1ch Draw
agreed.

White: Korchnoi
Black: Karpov

Moscow 1974
Final Candidates Match
5th Match Game

Queen's Indian Defence

1 P-QB4 N-KB3 2 N-QB3 P-K3 3
N-B3 P-QN3 4 P-KN3 B-N2 5 B-N2
B-K2 6 P-Q4 0-0 7 Q-B2 P-B4 8 P-Q5
PxP 9 N-KN5 P-N3 10 Q-Q1 P-Q3 11
PxP N-R3 12 0-0 N-Q2 13 N-B3 N-B2
14 P-QR3 B-KB3 15 P-K4 P-QN4 16
B-B4 N-N3 17 R-K1 P-QR4 18 Q-B2
B-N2 19 QR-Q1 P-N5 20 N-N1
B-QR3 21 P-KR4 R-K1 22 B-N5
Q-Q2 23 K-R2 PxP 24 NxP Q-R5 25
P-K5 B-KB1 26 QxQ NxQ 27 PxP
BxP 28 B-QB1 QR-N1 29 N-Q2 B-K7
30 N(2)-B4 BxR 31 RxB KR-Q1 32
NxB RxN 33 N-B4 R-KB3 34 B-B4
RxB 35 PxR NxP 36 R-N1 P-R5 37
P-Q6 N-K3 38 B-Q5 P-R6 39 NxP
NxP 40 B-B3 R-N5 41 P-Q7 N-K3 42
N-B2 R-N1 43 N-K3 K-B1 44 N-B4
R-N5 45 B-Q5 RxN 46 BxN K-K2 47
BxR NxB 48 R-Q1 K-Q1 49 K-N3
N-K4 50 K-B4 NxP 51 K-N5 K-K2 52
K-R6 N-K4 53 KxP N-B6 54 R-KR1
K-K3 55 K-N7 P-B5 56 R-R3 N-K4 57
R-R3 K-B4 58 R-QB3 K-K5 59 R-B1
K-Q5 60 P-B4 N-Q6 61 R-B1 K-K5 62
P-B5 N-K4 63 K-B6 N-N5ch 64 K-N5
N-K6 65 PxP PxP 66 R-B1 K-Q6 67
KxP N-N7 Draw agreed.

White: Karpov
Black: Korchnoi

Moscow 1974
Final Candidates Match
6th Match Game

Petroff Defence

1 P-K4 P-K4 2 N-KB3 N-KB3 3 NxP
P-Q3 4 N-KB3 NxP 5 P-Q4 P-Q4 6

B-Q3 B-K2 7 0-0 N-QB3 8 R-K1
B-KN5 9 P-B3 P-B4 10 Q-N3 0-0 11
QN-Q2 K-R1 12 P-KR3 B-R4 13
QxNP R-B3 14 Q-N3 R-N3 15 B-K2

15...B-R5 16 R-B1 BxN 17 NxB
BxPch 18 RxB NxR 19 KxN Q-Q3 20
N-N5 R-KB1 21 Q-R3 Q-Q1 22
B-KB4 P-KR3 23 N-B3 R-K1 24 B-Q3
R-K5 25 P-KN3 R-B3 26 Q-B5 P-N4
27 NxP PxN 28 BxNP R(5)-K3 29
R-K1 Q-KN1 30 P-KR4 R-N3 31 RxR
Black lost on time.

White: Korchnoi
Black: Karpov

Moscow 1974
Final Candidates Match
7th Match Game

English Opening

1 P-QB4 N-KB3 2 N-QB3 P-K3 3
N-B3 P-QN3 4 P-K4 B-N2 5 Q-K2
B-N5 6 P-K5 N-N1 7 P-Q4 N-K2 8
Q-Q3 P-Q4 9 PxPe.p. PxP 10 P-QR3
BxNch 11 QxB 0-0 12 PxQN4 N-Q2
13 B-K2 R-B1 14 0-0 B-R3 15 Q-N3
P-Q4 16 P-N5 B-N2 17 PxP BxP 18
Q-N4 N-N3 19 B-N5 Q-B2 20 KR-B1
Q-N1 21 N-Q2 N-B3 22 BxN PxB 23
P-N3 KR-Q1 24 N-B1 P-B4 25 N-Q2
Q-N2 26 P-QR4 R-Q2 27 P-R5

R(2)-B2 28 RxR RxR 29 PxP PxP 30
N-B4 BxN 31 BxB Q-K5 32 B-B1
R-B7 33 Q-N1 N-K2 34 Q-Q1 R-N7
35 B-N2 Q-B7 36 QxQ RxQ 37 P-R3
R-N7 38 B-B6 P-B5 39 PxP N-B4 40
R-Q1 N-K2 41 B-Q7 K-B1 42 R-R1
R-N5 43 R-R8ch K-N2 44 R-R7 K-B3
45 P-Q5 NxP 46 B-K8 RxBP 47
RxPch K-K4 48 RxP Draw agreed.

White: Karpov
Black: Korchnoi

Moscow 1974
Final Candidates Match
8th Match Game

French Defence

1 P-K4 P-K3 2 P-Q4 P-Q4 3 N-Q2
P-QB4 4 KPxP KPxP 5 KN-B3
N-QB3 6 B-N5 B-Q3 7 PxP BxBP 8
0-0 N-K2 9 N-N3 B-Q3 10 P-B3
B-KN5 11 N(N3)-Q4 0-0 12 Q-R4
B-R4 13 R-K1 Q-B2 14 P-KR3 B-N3
15 B-N5 P-QR3 16 B-KB1 P-R3 17
BxN NxB 18 QR-Q1 N-B3 19 B-Q3
B-R4 20 P-KN4 B-N3 21 Q-B2 BxB
22 QxB QR-Q1 23 R-K2 KR-K1 24
N-B5 RxR 25 QxR B-B5 26 R-K1
P-KN3 27 N-K7ch NxN 28 QxN
Q-N3 29 K-N2 K-N2 30 R-Q1 B-Q3
31 Q-K2 B-B2 32 R-Q3 Q-K3 33
Q-Q1 B-N3 34 R-Q2 Q-K5 35 P-N3
R-Q3 36 P-B4 P-KR4 37 RxP RxR 38
QxR QxQ 39 PxQ PxP 40 PxP K-B3
41 K-B1 K-K2 42 N-Q2 B-B2 43 N-K4
P-B4 44 PxP PxP 45 N-B5 K-Q3 46
NxPch KxP 47 P-N4 K-B5 48 N-B5
B-N3 49 NxP K-N4 50 N-B5 KxP 51
N-N3 K-R6 Draw agreed.

White: Korchnoi
Black: Karpov

Moscow 1974
Final Candidates Match
9th Match Game

English Opening

1 P-QB4 N-KB3 2 N-QB3 P-K4 3
N-B3 N-B3 4 P-KN3 B-N5 5 B-N2 0-0
6 0-0 P-K5 7 N-K1 BxN 8 QPxB
P-KR3 9 N-B2 P-QN3 10 N-K3 B-N2
11 N-Q5 N-K4 12 P-N3 R-K1 13
P-QR4 P-Q3 14 R-R2 N(4)-Q2 15
P-R3 P-QR4 16 B-K3 NxN 17 PxN
Q-B3 18 P-QB4 Q-N3 19 Q-N1 B-B1
20 B-Q4 N-B4 21 K-R2 B-Q2 22 R-N1
P-R4 23 R-N2 R-K2 24 Q-QB1 Q-B4
25 Q-K3 P-KB3 26 R-B2 K-B2 27
R-B3 QR-K1 28 R-KB1 K-N1 29
Q-B1 Q-N4 30 QxQ PxQ 31 R-K3
K-R2 32 R-KR1 K-N3 33 K-N1 N-R3
34 K-R2 N-N5 35 R-QB1 P-N5 36
P-R4 B-B4 37 K-N1 K-R2 38 K-B1
B-N3 39 K-K1 R-B2 40 B-KR1 K-N1
41 B-KN2 K-R2 42 B-KR1 Draw
agreed.

White: Karpov
Black: Korchnoi

Moscow 1974
Final Candidates Match
10th Match Game

French Defence

1 P-K4 P-K3 2 P-Q4 P-Q4 3 N-Q2
P-QB4 4 KPxP KPxP 5 KN-B3
N-QB3 6 B-N5 B-Q3 7 0-0 KN-K2 8
PxP BxBP 9 N-N3 B-Q3 10
N(N3)-Q4 0-0 11 P-B3 B-KN5 12
Q-R4 B-R4 13 B-Q3 P-KR3 14 B-K3
P-R3 15 KR-K1 Q-B2 16 P-KR3
N-R4 17 N-R4 N-B5 18 Q-B2 NxB 19
RxN B-R7ch 20 K-R1 B-B5 21
R(K3)-K1 B-N4 22 N(R4)-B5 NxN 23
NxN B-N3 24 N-Q4 BxB 25 QxB
KR-K1 16 Q-B3 Q-N3 27 R-K2 B-B3
28 R-Q1 R-K5 29 N-B5 QR-K1 30
N-K3 Q-K3 31 RxP B-N4 32 R-Q4
RxR 33 PxR QxQRP 34 N-B4 R-Q1
35 Q-Q3 P-N4 36 N-K3 Q-K3 37
P-Q5 Q-Q2 38 P-QN4 Q-Q3 39 Q-Q4
K-B1 40 Q-K4 BxN 41 RxB QxQP 42

Q-R7 P-B3 43 K-N1 Q-R7 44 K-R2
QxP 45 R-KN3 Q-B5 46 QxNPch
K-K1 47 Q-QN7 P-KR4 48 Q-B6ch
R-Q2 49 Q-B8ch K-K2 50 Q-B5ch
K-Q1 51 QxRP R-Q6 52 Q-R8ch
K-B2 53 Q-R7ch R-Q2 54 Q-B2ch
K-N2 55 Q-N3 R-Q5 56 Q-B7ch K-N3
57 Q-K6ch K-N2 58 Q-K7ch K-N3
Draw agreed.

White: Korchnoi
Black: Karpov

Moscow 1974
Final Candidates Match
11th Match Game

Queen's Indian Defence

1 P-Q4 N-KB3 2 N-KB3 P-K3 3
P-KN3 P-QN3 4 B-N2 B-N2 5 P-B4
B-K2 6 N-B3 0-0 7 Q-Q3 P-Q4 8 PxP
NxP 9 NxN PxN 10 0-0 N-Q2 11
B-B4 P-QB4 12 PxP PxP 13 KR-Q1
N-B3 14 Q-B2 Q-N3 15 N-Q2 KR-K1
16 Q-N3 Q-R3 17 P-K3 B-B3 18 Q-B2
B-R5 19 P-N3 B-B3 20 QR-B1 B-B1
21 N-B3 B-N2 22 B-K5 N-K5 23
B-QR1 QR-Q1 24 N-K5 Q-QN3 25
BxN PxB 26 Q-B4 Q-B2 27 P-QN4
RxRch 28 RxR B-B1 29 PxP B-K3 30
Q-R4 R-B1 31 B-Q4 P-B3 32 Q-R6
B-Q4 33 N-B4 Q-B3 34 QxQ RxQ 35
R-QB1 K-B2 36 P-QR3 R-R3 37 R-B3
K-K3 38 N-Q2 K-Q2 39 P-B3 PxP 40
K-B2 R-R4 41 P-K4 B-B3 42 KxP K-
K-K3 43 K-K3 R-R5 44 R-N3 P-N3 45
K-Q3 P-QR3 46 B-K3 B-N4ch 47
K-B2 P-B4 48 PxPch PxP 49 B-B2
B-N2 50 R-K3ch K-Q2 51 R-KB3
K-K3 52 R-K3ch K-Q2 53 R-KB3
K-K3 54 K-N3 P-KR4 55 R-K3ch
K-Q2 56 N-B3 K-KB3 57 R-K1 P-B5
58 N-K5ch K-B1 59 N-B7 PxP 60
N-Q6ch K-Q2 61 PxP R-KN5 62 NxB
PxN 63 R-KR1 K-B3 64 RxP B-Q5 65
BxB RxB 66 R-N5 R-K5 67 P-N4
R-R5 68 K-N2 R-KB5 69 K-B2 R-B6

70 K-N2 R-B7ch 71 K-B3 R-B6ch 72 K-Q4 R-B5ch 73 K-K5 R-R5 74 R-N8 RxRP 75 P-N5 KxP 76 P-N6 R-KN6 77 R-QB8ch K-N5 78 K-B6 R-KB6ch 79 K-K6 R-KN6 80 K-B7 K-R6 81 P-N7 Draw agreed.

White: Korchnoi
Black: Karpov

Moscow 1974
Final Candidates Match
12th Match Game

French Defence

1 P-K4 P-K3 2 P-Q4 P-Q4 3 N-Q2 P-QB4 4 KPxP KPxP 5 KN-B3 N-QB3 6 B-N5 B-Q3 7 0-0 PxP 8 N-N3 N-K2 9 N(N3)xP 0-0 10 P-B3 B-KN5 11 Q-R4 B-R4 12 B-K3 Q-B2 13 P-KR3 N-R4 14 B-Q3 N-B5 15 N-QN5 Q-Q2 16 BxN PxB 17 KR-Q1 N-B4 18 QxBP BxN 19 PxB NxB 20 PxN QxP 21 NxB Q-N6ch 22 K-B1 QxPch 23 K-K1 Q-N6ch Draw agreed.

White: Korchnoi
Black: Karpov

Moscow 1974
Final Candidates Match
13th Match Game

Queen's Indian Defence

1 N-KB3 N-KB3 2 P-Q4 P-K3 3 P-KN3 P-QN3 4 B-N2 B-N2 5 P-B4 B-K2 6 N-QB3 0-0 7 Q-Q3 P-Q4 8 PxP NxP 9 NxN PxN 10 0-0 N-Q2 11 R-Q1 R-K1 12 B-K3 B-Q3 13 QR-B1 P-QR4 14 Q-B2 P-QB3 15 N-K1 N-B3 16 B-B3 R-QB1 17 N-N2 P-R3 18 B-B4 P-B4 19 BxB QxB 20 PxP RxBP 21 Q-Q2 N-K5 22 Q-B4 Q-QB3 23 RxR PxR 24 N-K3 P-Q5 25 N-B4 Q-R5 26 R-QB1 N-N4 27 Q-B5

NxBch 28 PxN B-R3 29 N-Q6 R-K2 30 QxQBP P-Q6 31 Q-Q5 Q-QN5 32 K-N2 QxP 33 R-B6 Q-K4 34 QxQ RxQ 35 N-K4 B-N4 36 R-Q6 P-B4 37 N-B3 B-B5 38 P-B4 R-B4 39 K-B3 K-B2 40 K-K3 K-K2 41 R-QN6 R-B1 42 R-N7ch K-B1 43 R-R7 R-B4 44 P-KR4 P-R4 45 P-R3 B-R3 46 K-Q2 R-B3 47 R-Q7 B-B5 48 N-Q1 B-N4 49 N-K3 P-N3 50 R-Q5 R-N3 51 N-Q1 K-B2 52 N-N2 B-R3 53 N-R4 R-QB3 54 R-B5 R-K3 55 R-K5 R-QB3 56 N-B5 B-B5 57 N-R4 B-R3 58 R-B5 R-K3 59 R-B7ch K-K1 60 N-B3 R-N3 61 N-Q1 R-K3 62 N-K3 R-N3 63 R-B5 R-N7ch 64 K-B3 RxP 65 RxRP B-N2 66 KxP R-B6 67 K-Q4 K-Q2 68 N-B4 RxNP 69 P-R4 K-B2 70 R-B5ch K-N1 71 N-K5 B-K5 72 R-B3 R-N8 73 K-B5 K-B2 74 P-R5 R-QR8 75 K-N5ch K-Q3 76 P-R6 R-QN8ch 77 K-R5 R-QR8ch 78 K-N6 R-QN8ch 79 K-R7 K-Q4 80 R-B6 R-KB8 81 K-N6 K-Q5 82 R-B4ch K-K6 83 R-R4 B-R1 84 NxP K-B6 85 K-B7 R-Q8 86 P-R7 K-N5 87 R-R6 K-N6 88 R-R3ch K-N5 89 R-R5 R-QN8 90 R-R6 R-Q8 91 R-Q6 R-QR8 92 K-N8 B-K5 93 R-Q7 K-B6 94 R-KN7 R-R3 95 K-B8 K-N6 96 K-Q8 B-R1 Draw agreed.

White: Karpov
Black: Korchnoi

Moscow 1974
Final Candidates Match
14th Match Game

French Defence

1 P-K4 P-K3 2 P-Q4 P-Q4 3 N-Q2 P-QB4 4 KPxP KPxP 5 KN-B3 N-QB3 6 B-N5 B-Q3 7 0-0 PxP 8 N-N3 N-K2 9 N(N3)xP 0-0 10 P-B3 B-KN5 11 Q-R4 B-R4 12 B-Q3 B-N3 13 K-R1 P-KR3 14 B-K3 B-QN3 15 P-KR3 Q-Q3 16 B-K2 KR-K1 17 QR-Q1 Q-B3 18 N-R2 BxB 19 RxB

NxN 20 BxN Q-QB3 21 QxQ PxQ 22 R(1)-K1 BxB 23 PxB K-B1 24 N-B3 N-N3 25 P-KN3 RxR 26 RxR P-B3 27 K-B1 R-N1 28 R-B2 R-N3 29 K-K2 R-R3 30 P-N3 K-K2 Draw agreed.

White: Korchnoi
Black: Karpov

Moscow 1974
Final Candidates Match
15th Match Game

Reti Opening

1 N-KB3 N-KB3 2 P-KN3 P-Q4 3 B-N2 B-B4 4 P-B4 P-B3 5 PxP PxP 6 Q-N3 Q-B1 7 N-B3 P-K3 8 P-Q3 N-B3 9 B-B4 B-K2 10 0-0 0-0 11 QR-B1 B-N3 12 N-K5 N-Q2 13 NxB RPxN 14 P-KR4 N-B4 15 Q-Q1 Q-Q1 16 P-Q4 N-Q2 17 P-K4 N-N3 18 P-K5 R-B1 19 B-R3 P-R3 20 K-N2 N-B5 21 P-N3 N-R6 22 N-R4 N-N5 23 Q-Q2 P-QN4 24 N-B5 BxN 25 PxB N-B3 26 KR-K1 P-Q5 27 B-N4 Q-R4 28 QxQ NxQ 29 B-Q2 N-B3 30 B-KB3 P-Q6 31 R-K3 N-B7 32 RxP NxP 33 R-Q6 RxP 34 B-K4 R(1)-B1 35 R-Q1 N-B3 36 B-N5 P-R4 37 R-Q7 N(3)-N5 38 R-N7 N-Q4 39 BxN(5) PxB 40 B-K7 R(4)-B2 41 RxR RxR 42 B-Q8 R-Q2 43 BxP P-Q5 44 P-R4 PxP 45 PxP R-R2 46 B-N6 RxP 47 K-B1 Draw agreed.

White: Karpov
Black: Korchnoi

Moscow 1974
Final Candidates Match
16th Match Game

French Defence

1 P-K4 P-K3 2 P-Q4 P-Q4 3 N-Q2 P-QB4 4 KPxP KPxP 5 KN-B3 N-QB3 6 B-N5 B-Q3 7 0-0 PxP 8 N-N3 KN-K2 9 N(N3)xP 0-0 10 P-B3 B-N5 11 Q-R4 Q-Q2 12 B-K3 P-QR3 13 B-K2 NxN 14 QxN N-B3 15 Q-Q2 KR-K1 16 QR-Q1 QR-Q1 17 B-N6 B-B2 18 BxB QxB 19 KR-K1 P-R3 20 P-KR3 B-B4 21 B-B1 RxR 22 QxR Q-N3 23 R-Q2 B-K5 24 Q-K2 N-R4 25 Q-Q1 Q-QB3 26 N-R2 Q-QN3 27 N-B3 N-B3 28 N-Q4 N-K4 29 P-B3 B-N3 30 Q-K1 N-Q2 31 Q-B2 Q-R4 32 P-R3 Q-B2 33 N-N3 B-B4 34 N-Q4 B-N3 35 N-B2 N-B3 36 N-K3 Q-K4 37 P-QB4 P-N4 38 PxQP P-KR4 39 P-QR4 R-K1 40 PxP PxP 41 BxP QxN 42 BxR QxB 43 P-Q6 B-B4 44 R-Q1 Q-N4 45 Q-Q4 N-Q2 46 R-K1 B-K3 47 K-R2 Q-KN4 48 P-R4 Q-Q1 49 P-QN4 N-B3 50 Q-K5 N-K1 51 R-K4 QxP 52 QxQ NxQ 53 R-Q4 N-N2 54 P-N4 K-R2 55 K-N3 K-N3 56 K-B4 PxP 57 PxP P-B3 58 R-Q1 K-R3 59 R-Q4 K-N3 60 P-R5ch K-R3 61 P-QN5 P-N3 62 PxP KxP 63 P-N6 K-B2 64 R-Q2 K-K2 65 R-QB2 B-Q4 66 R-B7ch K-K3 67 R-R7 N-Q3 Draw agreed.

White: Korchnoi
Black: Karpov

Moscow 1974
Final Candidates Match
17th Match Game

Catalan Opening

1 P-Q4 N-KB3 2 P-QB4 P-K3 3 P-KN3 P-Q4 4 B-N2 PxP 5 N-KB3 P-B4 6 0-0 N-B3 7 Q-R4 B-Q2 8 QxBP PxP 9 NxP R-B1 10 N-QB3 Q-R4 11 R-Q1 B-K2 12 N-N3 Q-B2 13 N-N5 Q-N1 14 N-B5 P-QR3 15 NxN NxN 16 N-B3 N(2)-K4 17 Q-QR4 0-0 18 B-B4 Q-R2 19 B(4)xN NxB 20 Q-K4 N-B3 21 R-Q7 B-B3 22 QR-Q1 Q-N3 23 Q-B2 N-R4 24 R(1)-Q3 P-R3 25 P-QR3 R-B2 26 P-QN4 RxR 27 RxR R-B1 28 R-Q3

N-B5 29 N-K4 Q-B2

30 N-B5 N-K4 31 R-Q2 P-QN3 32 P-B4 PxN 33 PxN QxP 34 B-N7 R-B2 35 Q-K4 Q-R8ch 36 K-N2 QxP 37 PxP RxP 38 R-Q3 Q-R4 39 Q-B3 Q-N3 40 R-Q7 R-B4 41 Q-N4 Q-B7ch 42 K-R3 P-N3 White resigns.

White: Karpov
Black: Korchnoi

Moscow 1974
Final Candidates Match
18th Match Game

French Defence

1 P-K4 P-K3 2 P-Q4 P-Q4 3 N-Q2 P-QB4 4 KPxP KPxP 5 KN-B3 N-QB3 6 B-N5 B-Q3 7 0-0 N-K2 8 PxP BxBP 9 N-N3 B-Q3 10 B-N5 0-0 11 R-K1 Q-B2 12 P-B3 B-KN5 13 P-KR3 B-R4 14 B-K2 P-KR3 15 BxN NxB 16 N(B3)-Q4 BxB 17 QxB P-QR4 18 Q-B3 QR-Q1 19 QR-Q1 R-Q2 20 N-B5 NxN 21 QxN KR-Q1 22 R-K3 P-KN3 23 Q-B3 B-B1 24 R(K3)-Q3 Q-B3 25 N-Q4 Q-R5 26 P-R3 P-R4 27 R(1)-Q2 B-R3 28 Q-Q1 Q-B5 29 R-K2 Q-B2 30 N-B2 P-QN4 31 N-K3 Q-B4 32 R(K2)-Q2 BxN 33 RxB R-K2 34 RxR QxR 35 P-KN3 Q-K3 36 P-KR4 K-N2 37 K-N2

Q-K5ch 38 K-R2 Q-B4 39 K-N2 Q-K5ch 40 Q-B3 QxQch 41 KxQ K-B3 42 K-B4 R-K1 Draw agreed.

White: Korchnoi
Black: Karpov

Moscow 1974
Final Candidates Match
19th Match Game

Queen's Pawn Opening

1 P-Q4 N-KB3 2 B-N5 P-K3 3 P-K4 P-KR3 4 BxN QxB 5 N-KB3 P-Q3 6 N-B3 P-KN3 7 Q-Q2 Q-K2 8 0-0-0 P-R3 9 P-KR4 B-N2 10 P-KN3 P-QN4 11 B-R3 P-N5 12 N-Q5 PxN 13 BxB 0-0 14 B-N7 R-R2 15 BxQP P-QB3 16 B-N3 QxKP 17 Q-Q3 QxQ 18 RxQ N-Q2 19 R-K1 N-N3 20 P-R4 PxPe.p. 21 PxP P-QR4 22 R(Q3)-K3 B-B3 23 P-R4 P-B4 24 PxP PxP 25 N-Q2 K-N2 26 R-KB3 R-B2 27 N-B4 NxN 28 BxN R-Q1 29 P-B3 R(B2)-Q2 30 K-B2 R-Q7ch 31 K-N3 R-Q8 32 RxR RxR 33 B-N5 R-Q4 34 R-K3 R-K4 35 R-Q3 R-K7 36 R-B3 R-K4 37 K-B4 R-B4 38 R-Q3 RxP 39 KxP B-K4 40 K-N6 R-KN7 41 P-B4 RxP 42 R-Q7 P-N4 43 PxP PxP 44 P-B5 R-QB6 45 P-B6 P-N5 46 P-B7 P-N6 47 B-B6 BxPch 48 RxB

48...K-R3 49 R-B8 P-B4 50 R-B8 RxBch 51 KxR K-N4 52 R-N8ch K-B5 53 K-N5 K-B6 54 KxP P-B5 55 K-N4 K-N7 56 P-R5 P-B6 57 P-R6 P-B7 58 P-R7 P-B8=Q 59 P-R8=Qch Q-B6 60 Q-R2ch Q-B7 61 Q-Q5ch Q-B6 62 Q-Q2ch Q-B7 63 K-B3 K-N8 64 Q-Q1ch K-N7 65 Q-Q3 Q-QB4ch 66 K-N3 Q-N3ch 67 K-B2 Q-QB3ch 68 K-Q2 Q-KR3ch 69 Q-K3 Q-R5 70 R-QN8 Q-B3 71 R-N6 Q-B4 72 R-N2 K-R7 73 Q-R6ch K-N8 74 Q-QN6ch K-R7 75 Q-N8 K-R6 76 Q-KR8ch K-N5 77 R-N4ch K-B6 78 Q-KR1ch K-B7 79 R-N2 Black resigns.

White: Karpov
Black: Korchnoi

Moscow 1974
Final Candidates Match
20th Match Game

Ruy Lopez

1 P-K4 P-K4 2 N-KB3 N-QB3 3 B-N5 P-QR3 4 B-R4 P-B4 5 P-Q4 KPxP 6 P-K5 B-B4 7 0-0 KN-K2 8 B-N3 P-Q4 9 PxPe.p. QxP 10 R-K1 P-R3 11 QN-Q2 P-N4 12 P-QR4 B-N2 13 PxP PxP 14 RxRch BxR 15 R-K6 Q-Q2 16 Q-K2 P-Q6 17 PxP K-Q1 18 N-B1 R-K1 19 N-N3 N-Q5 20 NxN BxN 21 B-K3 BxB 22 QxB B-Q4 23 BxB NxB 24 RxRch QxR 25 Q-Q4 Q-Q2 26 P-R4 K-B1 27 K-R2 P-B5 28 N-K2 Q-B2 29 Q-K4 P-B3 30 N-Q4 Q-B3 31 NxNP QxRPch 32 K-N1 Q-K2 33 N-Q4 Q-B3 34 Q-B5ch QxQ 35 NxQ N-N5 36 P-Q4 N-Q6 37 NxNP NxNP 38 N-B5 K-Q2 39 NxP K-K3 40 K-B1 K-Q4 41 N-B5 K-K5 42 N-K7 KxP 43 NxPch K-K5 44 K-K2 N-B5 45 P-B3ch K-Q4 46 N-N4ch K-K4 47 N-B2 K-B4 48 K-Q3 N-K4ch 49 K-Q4 N-N3 50 K-Q5 N-R5 51 N-K1 N-N3 Draw agreed.

White: Korchnoi
Black: Karpov

Moscow 1974
Final Candidates Match
21st Match Game

Queen's Indian Defence

1 P-Q4 N-KB3 2 N-KB3 P-K3 3 P-KN3 P-QN3 4 B-N2 B-N2 5 P-B4 B-K2 6 N-B3 0-0 7 Q-B2 P-B4 8 P-Q5 PxP 9 N-KN5 N-B3 10 NxQP P-N3 11 Q-Q2 NxN 12 BxN R-N1

13 NxRP R-K1 14 Q-R6 N-K4 15 N-KN5 BxN 16 B(1)xB QxB 17 QxQ BxB 18 0-0 BxP 19 P-B4 Black resigns.

White: Karpov
Black: Korchnoi

Moscow 1974
Final Candidates Match
22nd Match Game

Catalan Opening

1 N-KB3 N-KB3 2 P-B4 P-K3 3 P-KN3 P-Q4 4 P-Q4 PxP 5 Q-R4ch QN-Q2 6 QxBP P-QN3 7 B-N2 B-N2 8 0-0 P-B4 9 R-Q1 P-QR3 10 PxP BxP 11 P-QN4 B-K2 12 B-N2 P-QN4

13 Q-Q4 R-QB1 14 QN-Q2 0-0 15 P-QR3 R-B7 16 N-K1 R-B2 17 BxB RxB 18 N-N3 Q-R1 19 QR-B1 R-B1 20 P-K4 R(2)-B2 21 RxR RxR 22 P-B3 Q-QB1 23 R-B1 RxR 24 NxR B-Q1 25 Q-B3 Q-R1 26 Q-Q3 N-N3 27 N-B2 N-B5 28 B-Q4 Q-B1 29 Q-B3 Q-Q2 30 N-Q3 P-KR4 Draw agreed.

White: Korchnoi
Black: Karpov

Moscow 1974
Final Candidates Match
23rd Match Game

Queen's Indian Defence

1 P-Q4 N-KB3 2 P-QB4 P-K3 3 N-KB3 P-QN3 4 P-KN3 B-N2 5 B-N2 B-K2 6 N-B3 N-K5 7 B-Q2 B-KB3 8 0-0 0-0 9 Q-B2 NxB 10 QxN P-Q3 11 QR-Q1 N-Q2 12 N-K1 BxB 13 NxB Q-K2 14 N-K1 P-B4 15 N-B2 QR-B1 16 P-N3 KR-Q1 17 P-K4 N-N1 18 KR-K1 PxP 19 NxP Q-N2 20 R-K3 P-QR3 21 Q-K2 N-B3 22 NxN QxN

23 R(3)-Q3 P-R3 24 P-QR4 Q-B4 25 Q-Q2 P-QN4 26 RPxP BxN 27 QxB PxP 28 R-Q4 Q-B2 29 Q-N4 P-K4 Draw agreed.

White: Karpov
Black: Korchnoi

Moscow 1974
Final Candidates Match
24th Match Game

Queen's Gambit Accepted

1 N-KB3 P-Q4 2 P-Q4 N-KB3 3 P-B4 PxP 4 P-K3 P-KN3 5 BxP B-N2 6 0-0 0-0 7 P-QN3 P-B3 8 B-N2 B-N5 9 QN-Q2 QN-Q2 10 P-KR3 B-B4 11 R-K1 N-N3 12 B-KB1 N-K5 13 NxN BxN 14 N-Q2 B-B4 15 R-B1 R-B1 16 Q-K2 R-B2 17 P-QR4 B-B1 18 B-R3 B-K3 19 Q-Q1 R-K1 20 N-K4 P-KB4 21 N-B5 B-B2 22 B-N2 N-Q2 23 N-Q3 R-QB1 24 P-QN4 P-QR4 25 PxP QxP 26 B-B3 Q-R2 27 P-R5 P-B4 28 Q-R4 N-N3 29 Q-R1 N-Q4 30 NxP NxB 31 QxN Draw agreed.

PROSPECTS FOR THE MATCH
by Michael Stean

The contrasting styles and temperaments of the two players promise to produce a fascinating struggle. In order to assess their relative chances it would be interesting to compare them in each of the three phases of the game: opening, middle and endgame.

Opening

Here Karpov has the edge. He is exceptionally well prepared and has a thorough knowledge of modern opening theory. Moreover there will be a strong team of Soviet theorists to back him up. Korchnoi of course has accumulated a vast background knowledge of theory over his many years as a leading professional, but is probably less *au fait* with modern theory than his opponent. He is very forceful in the opening, but there is always the danger of overpressing. Karpov on the other hand has a more sober approach to the opening. With the black pieces he generally has little interest in winning, but tries to equalize and steer the game towards a draw as quickly as possible. During the whole Candidates' cycle of 1973/4 Karpov won just two games with Black, and one of these only after a one move blunder on the part of his opponent. Karpov's match strategy is very clear: create an impregnable barricade with Black and pick off the wins with White. His opening repertoire with White is very powerful and he is heavily reliant upon it for his victories. For Korchnoi however White or Black make no difference. He plays to win.

So the battle in the openings will raise two questions:
Can Korchnoi find some breach in any of Karpov's iron defences with Black? Karpov is very, very solid with Black, taking not the slightest risk, but if his opponent over-extends himself in striving too hard for an advantage, punishment will be swift and lethal.

How well can Korchnoi stand up to Karpov's formidable prowess with the white pieces? The World Champion's power with White is a potential match-winner, but if it can be defused Karpov will be left in a terrible quandary. The flow of wins with White is his life-line, without which he will be forced to abandon his famous stability with Black and start to take risks.

Middle Game

Korchnoi is the deeper middlegame player, Karpov the more practical. The time factor will be crucial. Karpov plays good moves very quickly, Korchnoi plays very good moves slowly. The question will be whether Karpov can run his opponent into time trouble and force errors out of him, or whether the strength of Korchnoi's play can break up the champion's rhythm. If instead Karpov plays slowly and tries to match his opponent's depth of strategy then we shall see some wonderful chess - and some terrible time scrambles.

Endgame

The endgame is the acid test of any great player and here both contestants are supreme, but Korchnoi's greater experience must weigh in his favour. His knowledge and understanding of endgames is so intimate as to be almost instinctive, so that a series of long technical struggles would certainly favour the challenger.

Taking an overall and simplified view, Karpov holds the balance in the early phases of the game, while Korchnoi is somewhat stronger in the later stages. This would seem to predict a finely balanced struggle, but there is always an 'X' factor with Korchnoi. He can at his best bulldoze his way through any opposition, but is equally susceptible to disaster. Karpov's big chance is not to let him get into the match, but once Korchnoi has his foot in the door his capabilities are virtually limitless. There is also a second 'X' factor. Ever since Fischer-Spassky psychological warfare has become a regular feature of top-level chess, especially where there is an East-West conflict involved. The two sides are mutually suspicious of each other and both expect some kind of "trickery" to be used at some time or other with the result that any deviation from the accepted code of conduct, however slight, will probably receive the most sinister interpretation available. It remains to be seen who will take the first steps in this direction, but the tension will not be eased by the fact that Korchnoi is a defector from the Soviet Union and a sworn enemy of the State. For example, before his Candidates' Match with Polugaevsky in Evian, France, there were two days of negotiations and messages from Moscow to decide whether the Soviet player would be allowed to shake the hand of Korchnoi. (It is normal practice for players to shake hands before the start of each game). We can only speculate as to what kind of terrible contraption might have been concealed in Korchnoi's right hand to render the time-honoured practice so perilous. On the other side of the coin there was Korchnoi's violent reaction to Spassky's "box" tactics. During their recent Candidates' Match in Belgrade Spassky ceased to appear at the chessboard but insisted on sitting in a specially erected "box" behind Korchnoi's back, from where he would study the game from a large visual demonstration board. Korchnoi protested vociferously, but to no avail, and proceeded to lose the next four games! (He had previously been winning the match with considerable ease). Eventually Korchnoi recovered to win the match, but nobody has ever been able to explain the coincidence of Spassky's sudden unusual behaviour and Korchnoi's equally sudden demise.

It must be pointed out that Karpov has never to this date been involved in any of this "psychological warfare" and there is no reason to believe that he ever would be a willing party to any such an enterprise. But for propaganda purposes it is very important to the Soviet Union that the World Championship title remains in their hands. We can only await events and hope that the match will be played in a fair and sporting manner.

Intrigue and skullduggery aside, most people rate Karpov as favourite to retain his title. His tournament record and consistency make him a good choice for those wishing to invest money. It is probably Korchnoi, however, who has the greater depth of understanding of chess and the greater motivation. The format of the match, the winner will be the first player to win six games (draws do not count), probably favours the challenger slightly as it is he who has the greater capacity to win games. In their last match in 1974 there was a fixed limit to the number of games (24) and after establishing a lead early in the match (through superior opening preparation) Karpov was content to try and hold his advantage by drawing games until game 24. Such tactics would not work in this match as draws are irrelevant. In fact Korchnoi finished the 1974 match strongly, winning games 19 and 21 after trailing by three points, and almost managed to catch Karpov at the post. This would also seem to suggest that Korchnoi, despite being the older man, has greater stamina so that a long match might favour him. In any event both players have improved considerably since the last encounter and have done so in politically different halves of the world. Now they are set for the return match, the great showdown.

Steinitz
1886-1894

Lasker
1894-1921

THE GAMES OF THE 1978
WORLD CHAMPIONSHIP MATCH

Annotated by
Bent Larsen

GAME ONE
18th July

A quiet prelude. Korchnoi seemed annoyed when he left the playing hall while Karpov, satisfied with his first Black, stayed and discussed the game with Philippine officials.

But if Korchnoi wanted to play for a win, it must have been with himself that he was angry.

White: Korchnoi
Black: Karpov

Queen's Gambit Declined

1	P-QB4	N-KB3
2	N-QB3	P-K3

Inviting White to play 3 P-K4, which has been quite popular in recent tournaments. Miles and Timman play the pawn sacrifice 3 P-K4 P-B4 4 P-K5 N-N1 5 N-B3!? N-QB3 6 P-Q4, and each has drawn a game with the World Champion. Miles came close to winning, Timman almost lost, but one thing is certain, Karpov now knows that variation very well.

3	N-B3	P-Q4

Karpov often plays 3...P-QN3 here, but this time he wants a Queen's Gambit.

4	P-Q4	B-K2
5	B-N5	P-KR3
6	B-R4	0-0
7	P-K3	P-QN3

The Tartakower Variation; in the Soviet Union it is named after Bondarevsky and Makogonov. It has been an important part of the repertoire of Petrosian, Spassky and Karpov. In Spassky's match defeats against Fischer and Korchnoi his losses with this variation in game six

(Reykjavik 1972) and in game seven (Belgrade 1977) played an important role.

8	R-B1	B-N2

9	B-Q3

Did Korchnoi suddenly change his mind? Most spectators probably expected him to play, as against Spassky, 9 BxN BxB 10 PxP PxP 11 P-QN4!? But of course Karpov was prepared for this.

9 B-Q3 makes less sense than 8 B-Q3, with the idea to play 0-0, Q-K2 and KR-Q1 very quickly, asking the black queen where she wants to go.

9	...	PxP
10	BxP	QN-Q2
11	0-0	P-B4
12	PxP	NxP
13	Q-K2	P-R3!
14	KR-Q1	Q-K1

37

A good solution. Of course the queen will only stay here for a short time.

15	P-QR3	N(B3)-K5
16	NxN	NxN
17	BxB	QxB
18	N-Q4	KR-B1
	Drawn	

Further exchanges will soon follow, the pawn structure offers no problems, both positions are rock solid. So, Karpov got an easy draw with Black. He showed one of his prepared openings, which he can use both against 1 P-QB4 and against 1 P-Q4. Apart from that nothing happened - except one very important thing: the match got under way! In spite of political complications and personal antipathy the match had started, to decide the championship over the board and not at press conferences and committee meetings.

Capablanca
1921-1927

Alekhine
1927-1935
1937-1946

A duel begins. An opening duel. Most experts expected Korchnoi to play the French Defence - but look his king pawn went two squares! Then the open variation of the Ruy Lopez is not so surprising; Korchnoi has played it now and then for many years. But his 9th move is slightly unexpected. And move 11! I recommended that in 1966, in a booklet for ordinary amateurs.

Well, sorry, I guess that my 1966 book will look a little antiquated after this match.

White: Karpov
Black: Korchnoi

Ruy Lopez

1   P-K4   P-K4!?

Psychologically interesting. The French Defence served Korchnoi very well against Spassky, and also against Karpov in 1974. So why change? A very normal solid attitude would be: "I stick to the French until he refutes it!" But Korchnoi keeps the French (and the Sicilian, the Alekhine and all the others) in reserve, while he introduces a new problem: "Look, there is this rare variation of the Ruy. In my camp we have studied it very deeply. The books have very little to say about it, and they are full of mistakes. What do you know about this variation, Mr. Champ? If you do not know enough, you are free to get out on move 10, or 9, or 8, or maybe you would like to find another first move?"

2	N-KB3	N-QB3
3	B-N5	P-QR3
4	B-R4	N-B3
5	0-0	NxP
6	P-Q4	P-QN4
7	B-N3	P-Q4
8	PxP	

Of course, Karpov could play 8

NxP. Likewise, on the next move he might choose 9 Q-K2 or 9 QN-Q2, or one of the other reasonable moves. But he has his repertoire, and that means 8 PxP and 9 P-B3. Karpov knows his repertoire very well, but other variations not quite so well. And something else: this is like a poker game, and Korchnoi may be bluffing.

8	...	B-K3
9	P-B3	B-QB4!?

Old and well known. But 9...B-K2 used to be considered more solid, more positional, and that is the move which Korchnoi used to play.

10	QN-Q2	0-0
11	B-B2	B-B4!?

In 1966 this was completely forgotten. I wrote a small book about the Open Variation of the Ruy, where I recommended this line, simply because there was very little theory to learn. The books were full of 11...P-B4 and 11...NxBP?! and even 11...NxN. The treatment of 11...B-B4 in leading theoretical works of the time I summed up like this: "Keres shows sympathy, Euwe has little faith, Pachman considers this move weak".

Before the book was on the market (in Danish and German) I gave it good publicity by beating Fischer with the Open Ruy in Santa Monica. During the following years the variation was seen now and then, even from Grandmasters. Among Karpov's aides in Baguio, Igor Zaitsev may be the one who knows most about it.

12	N-N3	B-KN5
13	NxB	NxN
14	R-K1	

14   ...   P-Q5!?

New! Or as they write in *Chess Informant* and other books: "TN", meaning a theoretical novelty. Some TNs are of lasting value, others die a month later, or in the next issue or the next edition.

Normal has been 14... R-K1. That was my move against Fischer. An important variation in my book was 14...R-K1 15 B-B4 P-Q5!? 16 P-N4 N-K3 17 B-K4, which is favourable for White according to old analysis by the Russian master Rabinovich. I said that I could not see White's advantage after 17...Q-Q2, and as far as I know nobody else has seen it since. This was the first step in the rehabilitation of 11...B-B4.

Karpov played this opening with White against Smyslov in Leningrad 1977. After 14...R-K1 15 B-B4 B-R4 16 B-KN3 B-N3 17 N-Q4, he slowly got the upper hand. But later he almost lost that game (it was drawn after 69 moves) and that may have given Korchnoi the idea that Karpov did not feel at home in this type of position.

Is 14...P-Q5 good? Nobody knows yet. This game does not tell the answer! But it tells us that Korchnoi was not bluffing. He must have worked on this opening very seriously.

15	P-KR3	B-R4

| 16 | PxP | |

Not bad, but not a refutation either. 16 P-KN4 P-Q6 stinks; more interesting is 16 P-QN4, which is quite different from Rabinovich's variation. If the black knight goes to K3, it does not attack the white bishop. On the other hand, the white KP is less well protected, and in some lines the black QP forks White's rook and bishop. You are very welcome to analyze this on your own - we can all sleep when we get older. There are some interesting pawn sacrifices, and what about a piece sacrifice like 16 P-QN4 P-Q6 17 B-N1 BxN 18 PxB Q-Q4 19 PxN QR-Q1 20 B-B4 Q-B5... something like that. Stay at home, take a day off work tomorrow, and have fun!

16	...	BxN
17	QxB	NxQP
18	Q-B3	Q-Q4!!

Very good! Korchnoi must have prepared this move at home, where-ever that may be, Routine (read: bad) analysis would be something like 18...NxB (everybody is afraid of the bishops) 19 QxN(B2) N-K3 20 B-K3, followed by P-B4 with advantage for White.

White can now keep two bishops against two knights, but with a passive position. Sweet memories. (Find Fischer-Larsen, Santa Monica 1966 if you want to see a similar situation!)

Now 19 B-Q1 P-N5 and 19 B-N1 look satisfactory for Black, so Karpov decides to steer into an even ending.

19	B-K3	NxB
20	QxN(B2)	N-Q6!
21	KR-Q1	KR-Q1
22	QxP	

22 R-Q2 P-QB4 is bad for White.

22	...	QxKP
23	QxQ	NxQ
24	P-QN3	P-B3

The position is very open, so the bishop is supposed to be stronger than the knight. But the knight is well placed, and if White kicks it with P-B4 he weakens his position and places a pawn on a black square, which is something that he ought to avoid.

If White wanted to make a serious attempt, he should play 25 RxRch RxR 26 R-QB1, because the QB-file is far away from the black king. But it would be difficult to set Black any real problems.

25	B-N6	RxRch
26	RxR	R-QB1
27	R-Q2	P-KR4
28	B-K3	K-B2
29	P-B4	Drawn

There is very little play left after 29...R-B6!

GAME THREE
22nd July

At one point Karpov had used half an hour more than Korchnoi; an unusual and unpleasant situation for the champion. But the position was difficult, and just to avoid immediate disaster required exact defence. Afterwards several experts were sure that they knew where Korchnoi missed the win. He certainly had a promising position, but a clear win is not so easy to prove. I try at move 24.

White: Korchnoi
Black: Karpov

Nimzo-Indian Defence

1	P-QB4	N-KB3
2	P-Q4	

A strange move order. Most players feel that 1 P-QB4 gives Black more choice, for instance 1...P-QB4 or 1...P-K4. They may use the English Opening to avoid the Nimzo-Indian Defence, which is quite logical against a Nimzo specialist like Karpov. But here Korchnoi must have some other reason to move the QB pawn first. Or has he? Maybe it is like "Zukertort's Opening". Zukertort liked to play 1 N-KB3, but for no special reason. He continued with 2 P-Q4 and got positions he could also have reached with 1 P-Q4. Later 1 N-KB3 became "Réti's Opening", and deservedly so, because Réti played it as the beginning of a new system.

2	...	P-K3
3	N-QB3	B-N5
4	P-K3	P-B4
5	N-K2	

Korchnoi has played this before, and it has the merit of avoiding Karpov's pet line 5 B-Q3 P-Q4 6 N-B3 0-0 7 0-0 BPxP 8 KPxP PxP 9 BxBP P-QN3.

5	...	PxP
6	PxP	P-Q4
7	P-B5	N-K5
8	B-Q2	NxB
9	QxN	P-QR4!?

This may be new at this point, but it is a natural move. It is dangerous for Black to let the white pawn majority on the Q-side advance. In the 1973 Soviet Championship Spassky got a difficult game with Black against Korchnoi after 9...N-B3 10 P-QR3 B-R4 11 P-QN4 B-B2 12 P-N3.

The most common line has been 9...P-QN3 10 P-QR3 BxN 11 NxB PxP 12 PxP P-QR4, as in Reshevsky-Najdorf, Dallas 1957, and many later games.

10	P-QR3	BxN
11	NxB	B-Q2

This must be part of Karpov's preparation, which makes it difficult to argue against it. Still, I see no good argument against 11...P-R5. The bishop move is not necessary in all continuations.

12	B-Q3	P-R5
13	0-0	0-0
14	P-B4	P-KN3

White's Q-side majority is crippled, and he must seek his chances on the K-side. His good bishop and space advantage are important, but he has to be quick because Black will soon get play on the Q-side. Once the QN-file is opened the white pawn on QN2 will be a target.

Around here the analysis is extremely difficult. Black's last move weakens the dark squares, and in many cases White's P-B5 will be a strong pawn sacrifice. But P-B5 was a real threat, and 13...P-B4 is an ugly move, killing Black's central pawn majority.

15	K-R1	N-B3
16	B-B2	N-K2
17	QR-K1	P-N3
18	R-B3	R-K1!

P-B5 was a threat, but now 19 P-B5? NxP 20 BxN KPxB 21 NxQP Q-R5 gives Black good counterplay. In other critical lines the rook move creates a flight square for the Black king.

Against 18...PxP, 19 P-B5 would not have been good enough. But White would simply have recaptured, and after (18...PxP) 19 PxP B-B3 20 Q-Q4, he would combine threats on the K-side with a simple threat against the black QR pawn.

19	R(B3)-K3	B-B3
20	PxP	QxP

21 P-KN4!

21 P-B5 has been suggested, one of the points being 21...NxP 22 BxN KPxB? 23 NxQP! But first of all, 22...NPxB is quite good, with ideas like 23 R-R3 P-B3 24 Q-R6 R-R2 25 QxBP R-KB2 26 Q-N5ch R-KN2 27 Q-Q2 P-K4. And secondly, 21...NPxP 22 R-R3 N-N3 is unclear.

The only drawback of the textmove is the open position of the white king, which may give Black ideas like 21...QxNP 22 R-QN1 QxP 23 N-K4 PxN! But 21...QxNP? 22 P-B5! is murderous.

21	...	Q-B2
22	P-B5	KPxP
23	PxP	Q-Q3

23...Q-B5 looks more active, but a strong answer is 24 N-R2! The white rook is pinned, but so is the black knight, and the white knight gets to QN4 with unpleasant threats - except in the variation 24...K-B1 25 Q-N4!.

Each player now had about twenty minutes left. Experts were telling journalists about Korchnoi's fantastic position. So, after the game the journalists had some plausible questions for the experts. Since the game continuation makes it pretty clear that White's next move does not win, most hunts for improvements concentrated on this position. 24 R-K5 was suggested, and 24 R-N3. Both moves went to all corners of the world, "with a promising position", "with good chances" etcetera. Najdorf later stated that 24 R-N3 ought to win.

It is obvious that White has chances on the K-side, and that the black bishop is rather passive. But the open white king gives Black some chances, and it should not be forgotten that White's two Q-side pawns are neutralized by one black pawn,

and that the white knight is not taking part in the attack.

It is nice to study such a position some days later, late in the evening, alone, in peace and quiet. No chess clock, no hurry. I have spent more time on this position than the players on the whole game. I became interested when I could not find a win in the attack! 24 R-K5 is a nice-looking move with no special purpose, and even 24...NxP is tenable for Black. 24 R-N3 has something to be said for it; White tries to keep his BP and the threats connected with P-B6, but 24...K-R1! renews the threat against that pawn and makes N-N1 possible. Also, White has given up his pressure on the K-file. This pressure, and the lack of good squares for the black knight (except ...NxP) are two tactical elements in the position which do not necessarily indicate that White must win on the K-side.

I reached the conclusion that 24 PxP! is the right move and offers White very good chances to win - in the ending! Against 24...RPxP White has many good moves, for instance 25 Q-Q1, 25 Q-K2, 25 Q-B2 and 25 Q-N2. Even 25 N-R2. 24...BPxP 25 R-K6 is too ugly for words, so Black probably plays 24...NxP. Now 25 RxRch RxR 26 RxRch BxR 27 Q-K2, followed by BxQRP, ought to win, though there are many technical difficulties with the open king.

After 24 PxP! NxP 25 RxRch BxR there are several good moves. But first let us look at Black's pawns. He has four "islands", four isolated pawns! Also, Black may suddenly find himself in an ending with a bad bishop. The white knight, which never took part in the fun on the K-side, is very well placed, attacking two black pawns.

One of White's best continuations is 26 Q-N5. The ending after 26...Q-B5 27 QxQ! NxQ is very bad for Black, for example 28 R-KN1ch K-R1 29 R-N4 N-K3 30 K-N1 B-B3 31 K-B1. White activates his king while Black is tied down to the defence of his pawns.

Another interesting possibility is 26 Q-N5 B-B3 27 R-KB1 K-N2 28 N-K2! Suddenly White gets K-side ideas again, just because his knight gets to KB5 or KR5 with gain of time.

Conclusion: There is no mating attack, mainly because the white knight is not participating. But there is a lasting positional advantage, mainly because the black bishop is bad. Black's best practical chance would probably have been to give up the QRP at once: 24 PxP! NxP! 25 RxRch RxR!?

| 24 | R-R3(?) | NxP |
| 25 | BxN | PxB |

But not 25... RxRch? 26 QxR PxB 27 Q-R4 P-R3 28 QxP QxQ 29 RxQ, with a won ending.

| 26 | R-KN1ch | K-R1 |

| 27 | R-R6 | R-K3 |

| 28 | RxR | QxR |

After 28...PxR 29 Q-R6 Q-K2 30 N-K2 R-KN1 31 N-B4 Black has no winning chances, and in time pressure a knight is more dangerous than a bishop!

29	Q-N5	Q-N3
30	Q-R4	Q-K3
	Drawn	

Best play for both is 31 Q-N5 Q-N3.

I realise now that my recommendation on move 24 has the serious flaw that Korchnoi would have had to play on his birthday.

Both players received plenty of encouraging letters and also some pieces of good advice. An English farmer recommended a glass of milk before each game. He probably has something there; Miles drinks a lot of milk during his games - up to two litres. Karpov likes yoghourt. The more complicated Bobby Fischer got his milk in the form of mountains of cheese sandwiches.

A man from Pakistan recommended a certain opening variation to Korchnoi - adding that he had only learned the game a week before!

Korchnoi still has the initiative in the Spanish duel! He plays the same line as in game two, but does not care to see what Karpov and his aides have found against 14...P-Q5. Instead, he plays a well-known mistake!! The bluff is not called. Rightly so, for it was not a bluff. It was just one of those mistakes in the books.

White: Karpov
Black: Korchnoi

Ruy Lopez

1	P-K4	P-K4
2	N-KB3	N-QB3
3	B-N5	P-QR3
4	B-R4	N-B3
5	0-0	NxP
6	P-Q4	P-QN4
7	B-N3	P-Q4
8	PxP	B-K3
9	P-B3	B-QB4
10	QN-Q2	0-0
11	B-B2	B-B4
12	N-N3	B-KN5
13	NxB	NxN
14	R-K1	B-R4!?

What? The books quote Bronstein-Flohr 1944: 15 B-N5! BxN 16 QxB QxB 17 QxQP, with advantage, another point being 15...Q-Q2 16 B-K3 N-K3 17 BxPch! I even quoted this in 1966. Later it dawned upon me that the question mark should not be attached to 14...B-R4, but to 16...N-K3. After 16...N-R5! there is no sacrifice (17 BxPch? KxB 18 N-N5ch K-N3 19 Q-Q3ch Q-B4) and White must fight for equality! Korchnoi must have found the same variation.

15 P-KR3

A strange move, because the bishop had already gone away. Karpov probably played it to avoid Korchnoi's analysis.

15	...	R-K1
16	B-B4	N-K3
17	B-Q2	

Not 17 B-R2 N-N4.

17	...	N-B4

After White's passive play Black might try something: 17...B-N3 or 17...N-R4 or .... There is quite a large choice here.

18	B-B4	N-K3
19	B-Q2	**Drawn**

Well, Karpov is supposed to try for a win with White, isn't he? But so far Korchnoi has had an easy time with the black pieces, thanks to good preparation.

GAME FIVE
27th, 28th and 30th July

The Nimzo-Indian again, but Karpov soon deviates from game three. Korchnoi gets the two bishops, but an isolated centre pawn. Karpov gets a solid position - and inexplicably ruins it on move 37. This was the worst mistake in the match so far, but the next day Korchnoi gets into time trouble and throws away the win on move 55. Karpov sees his chance, sacrifices his last piece and draws thanks to the well known theme "bishop and wrong rook pawn". The last fifteen moves are rather superfluous, but make this the longest game ever in a title match.

White: Korchnoi
Black: Karpov

Nimzo-Indian Defence

1	P-QB4	N-KB3
2	P-Q4	P-K3
3	N-QB3	B-N5
4	P-K3	P-B4
5	N-K2	P-Q4!?
6	P-QR3	BxNch
7	NxB	BPxP
8	KPxP	

8 QxP avoids the isolated pawn but gives Black a lead in development after 8...N-B3.

8	...	PxP
9	BxP	N-B3
10	B-K3	0-0
11	0-0	P-QN3

12	Q-Q3	B-N2
13	QR-Q1	P-KR3

In a famous game Botvinnik-Tolush, White got the advantage after 13...N-K2 14 B-KN5 N-N3 15 P-B4! P-KR3 16 P-B5.

14 P-B3!?

This is probably new, and the idea may be to toy with B-B2-R4. But the most important quality of this move lies exactly in its novelty. It forces the opponent to think. In Reykjavik 1972 Fischer played many new moves in the opening, but most of these novelties were of little importance for opening theory. However, they gave Spassky a difficult time.

Probably best is 14 B-R2 or 14 B-B4, or 14 KR-K1 N-K2 15 B-B4, as Petrosian-Olafsson 1959.

Karpov's continuation looks a little passive, but he gets a solid position. A more aggressive idea would have been 14...R-B1 followed by ...R-B2-Q2.

14	...	N-K2
15	B-B2	N(B3)-Q4
16	B-R2	N-B5
17	Q-Q2	N(B5)-N3
18	B-N1	Q-Q2
19	P-KR4!?	

Korchnoi loves to gain space.

19	...	KR-Q1
20	P-R5	N-KB1
21	B-R4	P-B3
22	N-K4	N-Q4

There was a little threat on KB3. White has a free game, but it is not easy to attack the black position. During the next fourteen moves very little happens.

23	P-KN4	QR-B1
24	B-N3	B-R3
25	KR-K1	R-B3
26	R-QB1	N-K2
27	RxR	QxR
28	B-QR2	Q-Q2
29	N-Q6	B-N2
30	NxB	QxN

Two knights against two bishops, but still a very solid position.

31	Q-K3	K-R1
32	R-QB1	N-Q4
33	Q-K4	Q-Q2
34	B-N1	Q-N4
35	P-N4	Q-Q2
36	Q-Q3	Q-K2
37	K-B2	

37	...	P-B4??

Incredible! Not like Karpov at all. This move ruins his position completely and opens the game for the white bishops.

It looks as if this blunder was prepared with the previous move. Otherwise 36...R-B1 would have been natural.

38	PxP	PxP
39	R-K1	Q-B3
40	B-K5	Q-R5ch
41	B-N3	Q-B3

Against 41...QxRP, 42 R-K5! would be very strong, 42...P-N3 being unplayable because of 43 Q-B4 N-B3 44 Q-KB7.

42	R-R1!	N-R2!?

The sealed move. Maybe 42...N-K2 looks more plausible, but then 43 B-R4 Q-Q3 44 Q-K3 R-Q2 45 Q-K5 gives White a winning ending. So, Karpov's pawn sacrifice is not too surprising but Korchnoi and his seconds underestimated it and did not analyze it properly.

According to Stean you cannot keep Korchnoi out of time trouble! So, before move 49 he finds himself with less than two minutes for eight moves, and Lothar Schmid staring at that damned chess clock.

43	B-K5	Q-N4
44	QxP	Q-Q7ch
45	K-N3	N(R2)-B3
46	R-N1	R-K1

With the trick 47 K-R3? RxB.

47	B-K4	N-K2
48	Q-R3	R-QB1
49	K-R4	R-B8
50	Q-N3	RxR
51	QxR	

All very good, but as the old song said: "Give me five minutes more!"

51	...	K-N1
52	Q-N3	K-B2
53	B-N6ch	K-K3
54	Q-R3ch	K-Q4

And now 55 B-B7ch K-B3 56 Q-K6ch, the two easiest moves to see on the whole board (56...K-N4 57 Q-B4ch K-R5 58 Q-R6 mate).

55	B-K4ch??	NxB
56	PxNch	KxKP

56 moves made. But where is the win?

57	Q-N4ch	K-Q6
58	Q-B3ch	Q-K6

58...K-B7? 59 K-R3 Q-N4 60 Q-N2ch wins for White, but even 58...K-B5 offered drawing chances. After 59 Q-B1ch Q-Q6 some of the continuations are similar to the possibilities in the game.

Now 59 QxQch KxQ 60 K-N4 K-K5! 61 BxP N-B4 62 B-B8 N-K6ch 63 K-N3 N-B4ch is a hopeless draw, so White tries something else.

59	K-N4!?	QxQch

Not 59...P-N3? 60 QxQch KxQ 61 PxP NxP 62 K-B5.

60	KxQ	P-N3!

Not 60...P-N4? 61 B-B6 N-B4 62 P-Q5 K-B5 63 K-K4.

61	B-Q6	N-B4

Nothing was wrong with 61...PxP!

62	K-B4	

Hoping for 62...NxB?? 63 PxP N-K1 64 P-Q5.
62 PxP N-R5ch is a dead draw.

62	...	N-R5!
63	K-N4	PxPch

Not 63...P-KN4?? 64 B-B8, with an easy win.

64	KxN	KxP
65	B-N8	P-R4
66	B-Q6	K-B5
67	KxP	P-R5
68	KxP	K-N6!

Not 68...P-N4? 69 K-N5 K-N6 70 K-B5 KxRP 71 K-K5 K-N6 72 K-Q5 P-R6 73 K-B5, and White wins.

69	P-N5	K-B5
70	K-N5	KxP
71	K-B5	K-R3
72	K-K6	K-R2
73	K-Q7	K-N2
74	B-K7	K-R2
75	K-B7	K-R1

With the black pawn on QN4 instead of QN3, White would now play 76 B-B5 P-N5 77 PxP, and mate in three!

White cannot win by capturing one of the black pawns while the black king is in the corner. And he can only force the QNP to advance by a manoeuvre which lets the black king out.

76	B-Q6	K-R2
77	K-B8	K-R3

Not 77...K-R1?? 78 B-N8. And not 77...P-N4 78 K-B7 K-R3 79 K-B6 K-R2 80 B-K5 K-R3 81 B-Q4 K-R4 82 B-B5 K-R3 83 B-N6.

78	K-N8	P-N4

After 78...K-N4? 79 K-N7, Black gets too far away from his corner: 79...K-B5 80 K-B6 K-Q5 81 K-N5 K-Q4 82 B-N3 K-K3 83 KxRP etc.

79	B-N4	

A sad necessity. 79 K-B7 P-N5 80 PxP K-N4 draws at once.

79	...	K-N3
80	K-B8	K-B3
81	K-Q8	K-Q4

With the pawn on QN4 Black must stay away from the corner! Averbakh has shown that if the black king is confined to the corner QR1-QB1-QB3-QR3, White can force a win by stalemating the black king and com-

pelling the QNP to advance.

Here is an example (White: KQ6, BQN2, PQR3; Black: KQB1, PQN4, PQR5). White wins by 1 B-B6 K-N2 2 B-Q8 K-B1 3 B-N6 K-N2 4 K-B5 K-B1 (4...P-N5 5 PxP P-R6 6 K-N5 P-R7 7 B-Q4) 5 K-B6 K-N1 6 B-Q8 K-R1 (6...K-B1 7 B-B7 or 6...K-R2 7 B-B7 K-R1 8 K-N6) 7 K-N6 K-N1 8 B-B7ch K-B1 9 K-B6 P-N5 10 PxP. It is a paradox that without his two pawns Black draws easily if his king reaches the QR1 corner.

82	K-K7	K-K4
83	K-B7	K-Q4
84	K-B6	K-Q5
85	K-K6	K-K5
86	B-B8	K-Q5
87	K-Q6	K-K5
88	B-N7	K-B5
89	K-K6	K-B6
90	K-K5	K-N5
91	B-B6	K-R4

Adjourned again. Black's last move was rather confusing for the experts who had to give their newspapers a quick opinion. Why did he not play 91...K-B6.? Is there no danger if he is driven to his KN1? The danger should be a choice between being stalemated and going to QB1, where some losing positions are known.

Closer study revealed that Black could survive. So, the day after game six, there followed:

92	K-B5	K-R3
93	B-Q4	K-R2
94	K-B6	K-R3

Of course, not 94...K-N1? 95 B-B5 K-R2 96 B-B8 K-N1 97 B-N7 K-R2 98 K-B7.

95	B-K3ch	K-R4
96	K-B5	K-R5
97	B-Q2	K-N6
98	B-N5	K-B6
99	B-B4	

This position was analyzed by Averbakh in 1954. Black draws, even if he has to move. The funny point is that 99...K-N7! 100 K-K4 K-R6 101 K-Q5 K-N5 gets him to the Q-side in time, while 99...K-B7 or 99...K-K7 doesn't, though it appears to be the nearest way.

99	...	K-N7!
100	B-Q6	K-B6
101	B-R2	K-N7
102	B-B7	K-B6
103	B-Q6	K-K6
104	K-K5	K-B6
105	K-Q5	K-N5
106	K-B5	K-B4
107	KxP	

This means an offer of a draw. Without this pawn there are no tricks, Black can even allow his king to be stalemated. The position is rather simple to analyze, and this was done many years ago. White cannot win the last pawn without letting the black king into the corner.

107	...	K-K3
108	K-B6	K-B3
109	K-Q7	K-B2
110	B-K7	K-N1
111	K-K6	K-N2
112	B-B5	K-N1
113	K-B6	K-R2
114	K-B7	K-R1
115	B-Q4ch	K-R2
116	B-N2	K-R3
117	K-N8	K-N3
118	B-N7	K-B4
119	K-B7	K-N4
120	B-N2	K-R3
121	B-B1ch	K-R2

Equalling the record of Tal and Botvinnik (1961). But are all records worth beating?

122	B-Q2	K-R1
123	B-B3ch	K-R2
124	B-N7	Stalemate!

Korchnoi still hadn't offered a draw in this match!

When he was young, he was very interested in the theatre. But a slight speech difficulty kept him away from acting (though he did perform, and not without success, in a Russian movie about a chess grandmaster).

Which speech difficulty? Now we know. He finds it difficult to pronounce "Nitchya"!

Both players are tired and shaken by their mistakes in game five. According to Emanuel Lasker, when you have saved a lost match game you are in a strong position psychologically. But what if you got into that lost position with a blunder of a type you didn't know you had in you?

The opening is very similar to one of the games in their match in 1974. But on that occasion Korchnoi played White!

This game is a rest day for both players. But if the seconds have convinced themselves they know every little detail in the adjourned game, they ought to be working on the Ruy.

White: Karpov
Black: Korchnoi

English Opening

1	P-QB4(!?)	P-K4
2	N-QB3	N-KB3
3	N-B3	N-B3
4	P-KN3	B-N5
5	B-N2	0-0
6	0-0	P-K5
7	N-K1	BxN
8	QPxN	P-KR3
9	N-B2	R-K1
10	N-K3	P-Q3
11	Q-B2	P-QR4
12	P-QR4	

The bishop pair is not an advantage in this position. Not so much because the position is fairly closed at the moment, but because there are very few possibilities for White to open it! On the K-side this is due to the advanced black king's pawn. On the Q-side the doubled pawns are partly guilty, but even after that problem has been dissolved it is difficult for White to do anything. This is very clear after the text-move, which therefore is an indication of lack of ambition.

12	...	Q-K2
13	N-Q5	NxN
14	PxN	N-N1
15	B-K3	B-B4
16	P-R3	N-Q2
17	P-QB4	

Further reducing the mobility of White's Q-side pawns. But P-QN4 would not produce any serious threats, and the QP would be unprotected.

17	...	P-QN3
18	Q-B3	N-B4
19	P-N3	Q-Q2
20	K-R2	R-K2
21	B-Q4	P-KB3
22	QR-B1	Q-K1
23	Q-K3	**Drawn**

Black has won some small positional victories, but to go for the whole point would be very risky.

GAME SEVEN
1st August

An unusual variation of the Nimzo-Indian. Karpov plays a gambit; not his usual style, and Korchnoi likes to grab pawns! Later he exchanges it for an exchange, no pun intended. Karpov gets a strong pawn centre. Korchnoi has half an hour for the last dozen moves before the time control. Maybe that is too much? Several planless moves and two real lemons get into that dozen. But a miracle happens!

White: Korchnoi
Black: Karpov

Nimzo-Indian Defence

1	P-Q4	N-KB3
2	P-QB4	P-K3
3	N-QB3	B-N5
4	P-K3	0-0

The variation 4...P-B4 5 N-K2 is under repair.

5 B-Q3

5 N-K2 P-Q4 6 P-QR3 may suit Korchnoi's style quite well, but he has not played it often as White.

5 ...   P-B4

No doubt Karpov wants to reach his favourite line via 6 N-B3 P-Q4 7 0-0 BPxP 8 KPxP PxP 9 BxBP P-QN3. And no doubt the next move is a preparation by Korchnoi, inspired by a strong desire not to play as Karpov wishes.

6 P-Q5!?   P-QN4!?

Maybe even this is prepared? It looks more like Tal or Zaitsev than Karpov's play with Black, when he normally looks for equality. But maybe the champion considered Korchnoi's move so illogical that it must be punished drastically. Per-

haps he thought of Portisch's unsuccessful experiment against Donner in Beverwijk 1968: 6 N-B3 P-QN3 7 P-Q5 B-N2 8 P-K4 P-QN4?! Portisch's pawn used two moves to get to QN4, to go there directly looks better.

7	QPxP	BPxP
8	PxP	B-N2
9	N-B3	P-Q4
10	0-0	QN-Q2
11	N-K2	Q-K1

It looks like a Blumenfeld Gambit except for the position of the black king's bishop. (1 P-Q4 N-KB3 2 P-QB4 P-K3 3 N-KB3 P-B4 4 P-Q5 P-QN4!? 5 QPxP BPxP 6 PxP) The Blumenfeld is normally declined with 5 B-N5. Maybe Korchnoi would accept it?

| 12 | N-N3 | P-K4 |

53

13 B-B5

In similar positions, P-K4 is the way to break up the black centre. But 13 P-K4 PxP 14 B-QB4ch K-R1 is quite unclear here; Black's pieces are active.

13 ...   **P-N3**
14 B-R3   **P-QR3**
15 N-N5

Another idea was 15 PxP BxP 16 BxN, when Black loses a second pawn for unclear compensation. But after 15...RxP! there is probably compensation for the pawn, though 16 P-R3 B-R4 17 P-N4 proves that White has no difficulties.

15 ...   **PxP**

Almost forced. 15...Q-K2 16 P-K4 is good for White, for instance 16...P-Q5 17 N-K6 KR-B1(?) 18 P-B4!

16 N-K6   **P-B5**
17 B-Q2   **B-B4(?)**

18 N-B7?!

18 P-R4!? is very interesting, and for this reason I believe Black ought

to have played 17...B-Q3.

After 18 P-R4 RxP? 19 RxR PxR 20 QxP! Black is quite lost, and after 18...PxP 19 RxP! he is not much better off. After 18...P-Q5 19 RPxP RxR 20 QxR R-B2 21 P-N4! Black's centre collapses. Relatively best is 18...P-N5 19 NxN NxN 20 BxP Q-B3, but White is on top after 21 Q-B2. 21 P-B4?! PxP 22 RxP N-Q6 23 BxN NxR 24 PxN Q-N3ch! 25 K-R1 RxB is less clear.

18 ...   **Q-K2**
19 NxR   **RxN**
20 P-R3   **N-N3**

White has spent 75 minutes, Black 104. During the next moves Korchnoi takes it easy, probably underestimating the problems. He has often won games where he was the exchange up in return for some kind of positional compensation. One example was his first match game against Polugaevsky. "Polu" had a position it looked impossible to lose, but Korchnoi believed in his material plus and won, with some help from his opponent.

White must find a plan. Look at the position. Black has an impressive pawn centre. Apart from the fact that he has only a knight for a rook, what is wrong with his position? The answer must be that his king is not very well protected. Can White start something on the K-side?

Well, there is P-B4, which has the extra attraction that it attacks Black's centre.

The right move must be 21 K-R1. If 21...P-Q5, then 22 PxP PxP and now either 23 R-K1 or 23 P-B4. White is attacking already. Even 21...B-B1 (as in the game) 22 BxB RxB 23 P-B4 is very favourable for White. So Black will have to find a more quiet move. After most of these moves, the best continuation for both sides will be 22 P-B4 P-K5 23 N-K2. The black centre loses its mobility, and White has the advantage due to his material plus.

21	Q-B2?	B-B1
22	BxB	RxB
23	B-R5?	

Again, White ought to prepare P-B4. 23 QR K1 was good.

23	...	QN-Q2
24	Q-Q2	B-Q3
25	B-N4	

25 P-B4 PxP! 26 PxP N-B4 gives Black good chances.

25	...	N-B4
26	BxN	BxB
27	K-R1	Q-Q3
28	QR-Q1	

28 P-B4 still looks like the right idea. Then 28...N-N5 29 QR-K1 R-K1 30 P-R3 (30 P-B5 P-K5!) 30...PxP 31 PxP N-K6 32 R-B3 P-Q5 33 P-B5 or 33 N-B1 is in White's favour, though technically difficult.

28	...	K-R1

29	Q-B2	Q-K3
30	N-K2	Q-B3
31	P-R3	R-K1

32 P-QN4??

Maybe two question marks is one too many. But I have already seen the next move!

Why? Why? Why give Black such a strong passed pawn?

32	...	B-N3
33	Q-N2	

This means that the previous move was played without any idea. 33 P-QR4 is probably not good, but at least it was an idea!

33	...	K-N1
34	KR-K1	K-B2

35 Q-B2??

Very polite. First he said please to the bishop pawn, now he says it to the queen pawn.

The best move was 35 R-KB1!, and the answer would probably have been 35...K-N1.

35 ...   P-Q5

"Bolshoi spasibo". Thank you very much.

36	**N-N3**	**R-Q1**
37	**PxP**	**PxP**
38	**Q-Q2**	**P-Q6**
39	**Q-R6**	

A complete nervous breakdown. But the black pawns are too strong even after 39 R-QB1.

39 ...   P-B6
40 N-K4(!!)

A good try.

40 ...   NxN??

40...P-B7 wins easily.

41 QxRPch   K-B1

Adjourned.

The news went out to all continents. Karpov wins easily, or Karpov wins, or good winning chances for Karpov. Various experts were quoted. Time pressure is one thing chess players and journalists have in common, and chess masters working as journalists and journalists trying to be chess experts suffer from it too. I have always admired Donner for annotating my game in the 1964 Amsterdam Interzonal against Bronstein twice, two days in a row, in the same newspaper. The first evening he misunderstood everything, like everybody else.

So, I told readers of *Ekstrabladet* and *Expressen* that the black king goes to the Q-side, the win should not offer any problems.....

Next day Karpov arrived five minutes late. The envelope was opened. The sealed move was, of course.....

42 Q-R8ch   Drawn!

Karpov immediately offered a draw without making a move, Korchnoi accepted, the score sheets were signed.

"What's going on here?" shouted Robert Byrne from his seat. A happy smile was seen on Keene's face. Korchnoi got up from his chair with a strange expression on his face. Stunned, or just sleepy? He broke one of his rules and ordered a gin and tonic. Rules are broken on special occasions.

"By God, it's unbelievable!" Byrne could not believe it, but Keene showed him. Afterwards the chess editor of the *New York Times* called it a remarkable piece of analysis. He was now convinced that the position was a draw in all variations. Mikhail Tal said the same, Korchnoi, who has a way with journalists, explained that Karpov had been afraid he might have lost had he tried to win! He also said something about having a choice of three variations.

Let us see at least one variation. Otherwise we may create a rumour, something about that mysterious parapsychologist Vladimir Zoukhar, something about Karpov avoiding a scandal by giving a draw in a winning position! Earlier that day twelve rows of chairs had been removed, but after a protest from Baturinsky, less than half an hour before play was to begin, nine rows had been hurriedly installed again. All this was to avoid Mr Zoukhar's second row seat being too close to Korchnoi.

Was Zoukhar there to make Korchnoi nervous? What was Korchnoi afraid of? What would Korchnoi do if he had to face Zoukhar across the board??

It is much easier to analyze when you know what to look for! Here goes:

First we dispose of 42...K-B2 43 Q-R7ch K-B3 44 Q-R4ch K-B4 45 Q-N4ch K-K4 46 Q-N3ch!

So, we must try the Q-side: 42...K-B2 43 Q-R7ch K-K1 44 Q-R4? (or 44 P-B3? P-B7) 44...R-Q5 45 RxP RxR 46 RxNch K-Q2 and White has no way to continue. But 44 Q-R8ch and 44 Q-N8ch are still there.

I almost found a draw with (42...K-B2 43 Q-R7ch K-K1) 44 Q-R8ch K-Q2 45 RxPch K-B1 46 RxRch BxR 47 K-N1, but 47...Q-B3 48 QxQ BxQ seems to win. A miracle which does not work, even though it is inspired by game five, is this: 49 K-B1?! B-N4 50 K-K2 P-B7 51 K-Q3 P-B8 = Q 52 RxQch BxR 53 KxN BxP 54 K-Q5. Now Black can win in several ways, one is 54...K-N2 55 K-B5

K-R3 56 P-R4 B-N7 57 P-N4 B-B3 58 P-R5 PxP 59 PxP B-K2ch.

But that leads to the idea: (42...K-B2 43 Q-R7ch K-K1) 44 Q-N8ch! K-Q2 45 RxPch K-B1 46 RxRch BxR 47 K-N1!

After 47...P-B7?? 48 R-QB1 we get some kind of confirmation of Karpov's fears: he might lose. The black passed pawn is tremendous, but it cannot advance at the moment. There are also some threats against the white king, but he can defend himself in the best Steinitz tradition. Really, what can Black do? Against 47...K-B2, 48 RxN is probably good enough to draw, but 48 Q-N7ch! is simpler. And what can Black do after 47...N-Q7 48 R-QB1 (48...Q-B3? 49 Q-K8!)?

There is no win and so there is no reason to start that rumour.

During the 1972 match in Reykjavik, an Australian, living in South Africa, said he had such a gift for telepathy that he could beat Spassky and Fischer simultaneously! It made headlines for a few days. I have forgotten his name, but I would like to see a chess match between him and Mr Zoukhar!

GAME EIGHT
3rd August

Dr Zoukhar moved from the second row to the fifth, Karpov refused to shake hands, but an American journalist wrote about a boring match: too much rain and no Bobby Fischer! It must be a good guess that neither he nor his readers know much about chess. But rain is something most of us know. I am tempted to add that some of the best games in chess history have been played under such weather conditions. Rain is much better for chess than hot sunny days.

Maybe you are even interested in the game? It is a good game, by Karpov, and for the public. The public loves sharp attacks, and rightly so.

The game began with the Open Ruy and an unnatural tenth move by Korchnoi. Then a sharp pawn sacrifice by Karpov. After move twelve Tal told a journalist he would prefer to play White - so would most of us, after move 18 everybody. The black king remained in the centre and every woodpusher can enjoy asking: "why did he never castle?"

1-0. Korchnoi should have won game five, and maybe game three; he dominated the first six games. But Karpov should have won game seven. Well, we finally have a win, and officials and journalists begin hoping again. Home before Christmas!

Lothar Schmid has said that FIDE (the World Chess Federation) must change the rules before the next match, because the journalists feel condemned to chess for life. Very well said, but why does FIDE rule first and think afterwards? I was not the only one who called the rules insane before the match started.

White: Karpov
Black: Korchnoi

Ruy Lopez

1	P-K4	P-K4
2	N-KB3	N-QB3
3	B-N5	P-QR3
4	B-R4	N-B3
5	0-0	NxP
6	P-Q4	P-QN4
7	B-N3	P-Q4
8	PxP	B-K3
9	QN-Q2	

A natural developing move, played by the greatest before World War One. Recently it has been dusted off by Soviet grandmaster Sveshnikov.

9	...	N-B4

Recommended in the books. 9...B-K2 10 NxN PxN 11 BxB QxQ 12 RxQ PxB 13 N-N5 BxN 14 BxN R-KB1! did not give White any advantage in Sax-Tarjan, Hastings 1977-78. It is quite possible that Karpov would have played 10 P-B3 and been happy to avoid the variation 9 P-B3 B-QB4.

10	P-B3	P-N3?!

Classical theory gives 10...P-Q5 11 PxP NxQP 12 NxN QxN 13 BxB NxB 14 Q-B3 R-Q1 and, after 15 P-QR4, the equalizer is 15...B-N5!, which Lasker did not find against Capablanca in St Petersburg 1914.

10...NxB 11 NxN B-K2 12 N(B3)-Q4 is unpleasant for Black. After 12...NxN 13 PxN he has a hole on QB4, and after 12...NxP 13 R-K1

N-N3 14 NxB PxN 15 N-Q4 (Kuzmin-Belyavsky) Black's position didn't last long.

But why not the classical solution? Is the resulting position not complicated enough for Korchnoi? Maybe, or perhaps he just wanted to keep the psychological initiative with a new surprise in the Spanish duel. Then again it is possible that he didn't like 10...P-Q5 11 BxB NxB 12 N-N3 PxP 13 Q-B2, a suggestion by Sveshnikov.

P-N3 is known in some variations of the Open Ruy. The main idea is pressure against the white KP. An unpleasant detail is that the black bishop does not control the ...QB4 square.

White might get the idea of sacrificing at once with 11 N-Q4, but the consequences are unclear. Korchnoi may well have analyzed this. Karpov finds something more subtle.

| 11 | Q-K2(!) | B-N2 |
| 12 | N-Q4 | NxP |

Logical, but very risky. The emergency exit was 12...N-K2 13 P-KB4 Q-Q2, but with the KP well protected the black fianchetto bishop loses much of its charm. A likely continuation is 14 B-B2 0-0 (14...N-N2,

to play ...P-QB4, is bad because of 15 P-QR4!) 15 P-QN4 and the black position looks unpleasant.

13	P-KB4	N-B5
14	P-B5	PxP
15	NxBP	R-KN1

It is easy to suggest 15...B-KB1, but it is difficult to like Black's position.

| 16 | NxN | QPxN(?) |

In similar positions this idea is known; take with the QP and stop White's attack with ...N-Q6. But here it does not stop the attack, and the black king cannot get away from the centre. It may be possible to prove that 16...NPxN holds out longer, but the position is full of holes and the king cannot hide anywhere, so there is no real hope.

17 B-B2   N-Q6?

Korchnoi is famous for brilliant defence and counter-attack in difficult positions; he calculates more and better than most leading grandmasters. But did he see White's next move? Or had he resigned already?

White is threatening 18 NxBch RxN 19 Q-K5 (17 NxBch RxN 18 Q-K5 RxPch! was unclear) and Black's only chance was 17...Q-Q4! One of the ideas is 18 NxBch RxN 19 B-R6 R-N3! If White takes the exchange, Black has a pawn for it and quite an active position. After 20 QR-Q1 N-Q6 21 BxN PxB 22 RxP White certainly stands better, but Black is still fighting.

18 B-R6!

Decisive. White gains time to mobilize his queen's rook. 18...BxB 19 NxB R-KB1 20 NxP Q-K2 21 Q-K4 is very sad, and to have some fun you should look at 20 RxP RxR 21 QxBch R-K2 22 Q-QB6ch R-Q2 23 R-KB1 from White's side of the board.

18	...	B-KB1
19	QR-Q1	Q-Q4
20	BxN	PxB
21	RxP	Q-B3

Material is equal, but all White's pieces take part in the attack and the black king cannot escape. The end may come at any moment.

22 BxB   Q-N3ch

Or 22...KxB 23 N-Q4. Against 22...RxB there are many quick wins, I like 23 N-N7ch K-K2 24 Q-KB2 Q-N3 25 R-Q4. When you see how much enthusiasm many chess players show while working on positions like this, you may get the terrible idea that necrophilia is natural.

| 23 | K-R1 | KxB |
| 24 | ·Q-B3 | |

24 ...   R-K1(?)

24...R-N1 would have prolonged the agony, but not by much, for instance 25 N-R6 R-KN2 26 Q-KB6 P-B4 27 R(B1)-Q1 or, a more beautiful variation, 25 N-R6 R-KN2 26 Q-KB6 R-N3 27 R-Q8ch RxR 28 QxR(Q8)ch K-N2 29 RxPch!! and mate next move.

25	N-R6	R-N2
26	R-Q7!	

26	...	R-QN1

26...BxR 27 QxPch is too beautiful!

27	NxP	BxR
28	N-Q8ch!	Resigns

Well played by Karpov, and a nice finish. Thanks on behalf of my readers; they get tired of a series of draws.

I have been told that when Spassky played his first match against Petrosian he felt that he did not know how he could win a game. Botvinnik then gave him the surprising advice: lose one!

In the Danish chess magazine *Skakbladet* editor Rosenlund assured his readers that Dr Zoukhar was as harmless as Santa Claus.

In *Schakend Nederland* a reader could not understand what all the fuss was about. There are rules! Why haven't they disqualified either Korchnoi or both?

Euwe
1935-1937

Botvinnik
1948-1957
1958-1960
1961-1963

From the English Opening transposition into the Queen's Gambit, as in game one. But White varies on move five. Both sides follow known master games up to move 14 where Karpov tries a new move. It may be a preparation, but it does not look very good. In the continuation White easily obtains a small but clear positional advantage. Either something went wrong for the world champion in connection with move 14, or maybe he is confident that he can hold a slightly inferior position?

It is easy to suggest small improvements on Black's play, but nothing really changes the valuation of the position. However, Korchnoi uses too much time. If he had had a couple of minutes for the last couple of moves he would have won. His 39th move had very little to do with master chess.

White: Korchnoi
Black: Karpov

Queen's Gambit Declined

1	P-QB4	N-KB3
2	N-QB3	P-K3
3	N-B3	P-Q4
4	P-Q4	B-K2
5	B-B4	

5	...	0-0
6	P-K3	P-B4
7	QPxP	BxP
8	Q-B2	N-B3
9	R-Q1	Q-R4
10	P-QR3	B-K2
11	N-Q2	P-K4
12	B-N5	P-Q5
13	N-N3	Q-Q1
14	B-K2	

Maybe Korchnoi does not want to discuss the Tartakower Variation. Perhaps he is keeping something in store for a more critical phase of the match.

As for the next few moves: this is not a book on opening theory!

14	...	P-KR3?

14...N-KN5 15 BxB QxB 16 PxP Q-R5 is interesting. In Petrosian-Filip, Curacao 1962, White came out of the complications with the advantage, in Portisch-Spassky, Havana

1966, Black equalized. Improvements may still be found.

The text move avoids these complications, but that is not enough to make it a good move.

15	BxN	BxB
16	0-0	B-K3
17	N-B5	Q-K2
18	NxB	QxN
19	N-Q5	QR-Q1

19...QR-B1 or 19...B-Q1 cannot alter the impression that White is building a strong position. The knight on Q5 will not last forever, but the pawn majority on the Q-side ought to be of lasting value.

20	B-Q3	N-K2

21 NxBch

Even 21 B-K4 gives White the advantage, but with opposite coloured bishops Black can hope for a draw.

21	...	QxN
22	PxP	PxP

22...RxP is not better. White plays either 23 B-K4 or 23 B-R7ch K-R1 24 RxR PxR 25 B-Q3 followed by R-K1.

23	KR-K1	R-Q2
24	R-K4	N-B3
25	Q-K2	P-KN3

Both players seem to agree that Black has no time for ...P-QR4. Or maybe they agree that 26 P-QN4 P-QR4 (27 P-N5 N-Q1) does not increase White's advantage.

26	R-K1	K-N2
27	P-QN4	P-N3

27...P-QR4 would be countered by the strong 28 Q-N4!, the simple point being that 28...KR-Q1 occupies the square the knight wanted. After 29 P-N5 N-K2 30 P-B5 the black position would be just as difficult as in the game.

28	Q-N4	KR-Q1
29	P-KR4	P-KR4
30	Q-N3	Q-Q3(?)

To weaken the position of the white king. In a bad position an understandable idea. But P-B4 is also an attacking move. Objectively, 30...P-R4 was better.

31	P-B4	R-K2

31...P-R4 32 P-N5 N-K2 33 R-K5

(33...QxP 34 P-KB5!) looks rather horrible.

32	RxR	NxR
33	R-K5	

Black is on the ropes. Q-side pawn majority, K-side attack, the only open file; White has everything. Black's only consolation is his passed pawn, but the white bishop is, in this position, an ideal blockader, combining its defensive job with threats against the black king.

But Korchnoi has no time .....

33	...	P-R4!?

33...K-R1 and 33...K-B1 are hopeless after 34 Q-N5. 33...R-KR1 is too passive, a good answer is 34 K-R2, preparing P-KB5.

33...P-B3 looks bad, but 34 P-QB5 PxP 35 PxP Q-B2 36 RxNch QxR 37 QxPch K-B1 38 Q-R6ch Q-N2 39 QxRP Q-N6 is not convincing, better simply 34 RxP.

33...P-B4 looks better. 34 BxP is unclear, but 34 Q-N5 R-Q2 35 P-B5 PxP 36 PxP Q-KB3 37 B-N5 R-N2 38 QxQch KxQ 39 B-B4 R-B2 40 K-B2 is a difficult ending for Black.

34	RxKRP	

34 PxP PxP 35 RxQRP R-QN1 is unclear.

34	...	PxP
35	PxP	QxNP
36	R-QN5(?)	

36 R-K5! was the precise move: 36...Q-Q3 37 P-R5 or 36...N-B3 37 R-KN5, with decisive threats.

36	...	Q-Q7
37	K-R2	Q-K6
38	RxP	R-QR1?

38...QxQch 39 KxQ N-B4ch! offered some drawing chances.

39	QxQ??	PxQ
40	R-N2	R-R6
41	B-K4	R-B6
42	Drawn	

41...R-B6 was the sealed move.

Back to the diagram: 39 Q-N5 ought to win, for instance 39...QxB 40 QxN QxP 41 P-R5 PxP 42 Q-N5ch K-B1 43 R-KR6. Or (39 Q-N5 QxB 40 QxN) 40...Q-B4 41 Q-Q6 P-Q6 42 Q-Q4ch K-N1 43 R-N3, winning a second pawn (43...Q-N5 44 RxP QxRPch 45 R-R3 R-Q1 46 Q-K5).

That would have been a fitting conclusion to White's fine play, which really aimed at the black king during most of the game. The attack grew out of White's control of the only open file and his excellent blockader on Q3, the bishop stopping the black pawn and at the same time taking part in the action on the K-side. Instead, 39 QxQ shows very well why you should always have five minutes for the last move before the time control.

When Korchnoi had accepted the draw offer he commented: "Not very polite, to offer a draw a pawn down." I don't agree. Offering a draw, revealing your sealed move, can never be impolite. The point is that even in a dead drawn position it is difficult for your opponent to offer a draw. After all, you might have sealed a very bad move, or even an illegal move!

Mr Zoukhar had now been moved back to the seventh row. Korchnoi's aides tried to get him seated together with the other Russians in the gallery. It seems that Lothar Schmid had given the organizers some kind of advice in that direction. Karpov protested; a handwritten note said, among other things: "It is with regret that I must note these, as well as some other actions on the part of the chief arbiter, generate doubts as to his objectiveness and impartiality."

The Russians said Zoukhar was an expert on psychology and neurology, and that he wanted to study psychological conditions in the playing hall and Korchnoi's behaviour.

The jury decided 3-2 to support Karpov's view and keep Zoukhar where he was on this day, row seven. This was called an emergency meeting and lasted five hours. But some sources said Korchnoi was getting over his Zoukhar fright. And Karpov said he did not intend to behave like a sportsman when his opponent was concocting scandal stories against him, particularly concerning Zoukhar.

All in all, if you are a chess fan, you should not let it be known that you are interested in parapsychology.

GAME TEN
8th August

This commentator is not sure that Korchnoi's endgame play is better than Karpov's. At least not in general, although in this game it was! Karpov got a small endgame advantage - and found himself struggling for a draw!

But the game will mainly be remembered for White's 11th move. A bomb! An improvement on opening theory which has been valid (or at least copied, from book to book) since 1914.

"That move must have been found by Tal!", said one of my friends. I probably agreed, but basically I disagree. If a strong player analyzes a position in depth, the outcome is not a question of style. If Petrosian analyzes a position where the strongest move is "typical Tal", the result of the analysis will be that move. In this case, the discoverer may be Karpov, Balashov, Zaitsev, Tal or somebody else. Like Sveshnikov, who has reintroduced the Bernstein variation 9 QN-Q2, probably not without a little homework.

The move was good, even brilliant, surprising, sensational and so on. Korchnoi could not refute it, but he found something playable. He survived the shock and got a probably tenable ending. Well done, but where is the initiative in the Spanish duel now?

White: Karpov
Black: Korchnoi

Ruy Lopez

1	P-K4	P-K4
2	N-KB3	N-QB3
3	B-N5	P-QR3
4	B-R4	N-B3
5	O-O	NxP
6	P-Q4	P-QN4
7	B-N3	P-Q4
8	PxP	B-K3
9	QN-Q2	N-B4
10	P-B3	P-Q5

The book move. The surprise 10...P-N3?! backfired in game 8.

11 N-N5!?

I don't say sorry! But I confess, I am one of many authors who have written about this opening without seeing this move. Probably somebody even saw it and kept his secret?

Is it typical Tal? Oh no! Because it is not an unclear piece sacrifice. After 11...QxN 12 Q-B3 K-Q2 13 B-Q5! White just wins back the piece with advantage. The sacrifice 13...NxP!? 14 BxBch NxB 15 QxR N-KB5 is not good enough. And 12...B-Q2 13 BxPch K-Q1 14 PxP is unplayable for Black.

This is Karpov's first important innovation in the match. But why did he not try to get it in before, in game

66

2, 4 or 6? There are several possible explanations: either the Russians found it later; or they kept this shocker in store for a really important game; or they had other nice surprises ready, in variations Korchnoi avoided.

11	...	PxP
12	NxB	KBPxN
13	PxP	Q-Q6!

Avoids White's Q-B3. 14 B-B2 QxP 15 Q-R5ch P-N3 is bad for White.

14	N-B3	QxQ
15	BxQ	B-K2
16	B-K3	N-Q6
17	B-N3	K-B2
18	QR-Q1	N(Q6)xKP

Not 18...QR-Q1 19 N-N5ch.

19	NxNch	NxN
20	B-KB4	N-B5
21	BxN	PxB
22	R-Q4(?)	

Both R-Q7 and BxP look much better. Black is probably able to draw, but he would have to play well.

22	...	B-Q3!

After 23 BxB PxB 24 RxQP KR-Q1 Black draws easily.

23	B-K3	KR-QN1
24	RxP	R-N7
25	P-QR4	R-R7
26	P-N3	R-QN1

Black is active and not in danger of losing, though he has three isolated pawns.

27	R-Q1	R(N1)-N7

Better than 27...R-N6 28 B-B5.

White ought to play 28 K-N2.

28	R(Q1)-Q4?	R-N8ch
29	K-N2	R(N8)-QR8
30	R-R4	P-R3
31	B-B5	P-K4!

Karpov must have overlooked 32 BxB PxB 33 R-B6 R-Q8 34 RxQRP R(Q8)-Q7.

32	B-R7	K-K3
33	R(B4)-KN4	

33 R(R4)-N4 K-Q4 34 R(B4)-K4 R-B7 gives Black good chances.

33	...	B-K2
34	R-R5	B-B3
35	R-QB4	K-Q2

35...RxRP 36 RxBP R-QB8 was also quite promising.

36	B-N8	P-B3
37	R-K4	

37 BxP? P-N3.

37	...	RxRP
38	P-QB4	

38	...	R-R4

38...R-QB8 39 BxP R(B8)xP 40 RxR RxR 41 BxB PxB 42 RxP offers Black no winning chances.

39	BxP	BxB(?)

39...R-QB8 40 B-B4 RxR 41 BxR P-R4 or 39...R(R8)-R5 may be a draw, but White would have to defend very carefully.

40	R(R5)xB	RxR
41	RxR	R-R5
42	R-K4	

Even 42 P-R4 was good (42...RxP 43 R-QR5)

42	...	R-R4
43	P-R4	P-R4
44	R-B4	Drawn

Karpov's offer went via the referee. The players were not on speaking terms.

A not very surprising surprise on move one, then passive play by Karpov, weak play by Karpov, and a blunder by Karpov. A very easy win for Korchnoi. And really a rather uninteresting game, except for the result and all its match-tactical and psychological consequences. The score is even, and the way it happened must shake the champion's self-confidence.

The opening was not "typical Korchnoi", but the sequel was. He loves to gain space, which he did quite early here. He has faith in the bishop pair. It was a well planned, well played game and therefore a well deserved victory - but against weak opposition. The match has still to produce a really fine win, a victory against good defence.

White: Korchnoi
Black: Karpov

Sicilian Defence

1   P-KN3   P-QB4

Karpov pondered for five minutes. With the text move he may have been hoping for a symmetrical English, after an early P-QB4 by White.

The surest way to stay "within his repertoire" would have been 1...P-Q4, which Korchnoi normally answers by 2 N-KB3. This might have led to Réti or Catalan positions which were seen in the 1974 match.

Korchnoi has played 1 P-KN3 many times. He may have chosen it against Karpov for the simple reason that it makes it difficult for Black to get into the main line of the Queen's Indian, one of Karpov's favourite defences not only after 1 P-Q4, but even in many cases after 1 N-KB3 or 1 P-QB4.

2   B-N2   N-QB3
3   P-K4!

Now we may call the opening a Sicilian, which Karpov does not like to play with Black. But of course it is a rather strange Sicilian. 3...P-K3

would have been psychologically interesting, because many years ago it was Korchnoi who made Spassky lose most of his sympathy for the Closed Sicilian with 1 P-K4 P-QB4 2 N-QB3 P-K3!?

3   ...   P-KN3
4   P-Q3   B-N2
5   P-KB4

White plays a Closed Sicilian, but postponing N-QB3. This "semi-Dutch" system has been more popular with Black, against 1 P-QB4. White's extra move must be useful, and at least there is very little exact theory.

5   ...   P-Q3

6	N-KB3	N-B3
7	O-O	O-O
8	P-B3	

Definitely dropping the idea of N-B3. Both sides have flexible positions which may result in many different pawn structures in the centre.

8	...	R-N1
9	Q-K2	N-K1

Rather passive. An interesting idea is 9...B-N5 followed by ...N-Q2, ...Q-B2 and the advance of the QN-pawn. The exchange of White's king's knight makes it more difficult for him to advance in the centre.

10	B-K3	N-B2
11	P-Q4	PxP
12	PxP	B-N5
13	R-Q1	P-Q4
14	P-K5	

It has been said that P-Q5 is Korchnoi's favourite move. But P-K5, hemming in an enemy fianchetto bishop, is not bad either.

14	...	Q-Q2
15	N-B3	KR-B1
16	Q-B1!	P-QN4(?)

The most obvious effect of this nervous move is that Black gets a hole on QB4. It was probably better to try to conquer some squares on the Q-side with pure piece play, as in some variations of the French Defence, jumping here and there with the knights. One idea is ...N-R1-N3(-B5). But maybe it is best to gain some space on the K-side first, with ...P-KB4. (All of which should not hide the fact that White has a slight edge).

17	P-KR3	BxN

Like a good boy. 17...P-N5!? was more interesting.

18	BxB	P-N5(?)
19	B-N4!	P-K3

20 N-R4   N-R4

To understand the previous comment readers should note that with the white bishop on KB3 Black would have 20...NxQP or 20...NxKP here.

21	N-B5	Q-K1
22	B-K2	N-N2
23	NxN	RxN
24	R(Q1)-B1!	

They say you always move the wrong rook. This is the exception, but Korchnoi could not dream of the game continuation where his choice of rook becomes decisive.

24	...	Q-Q2
25	R-B2!	P-N6??

A blunder, turning a slightly difficult position into an absolutely lost one. 25...R(N2)-N1 was natural, even 25...B-B1 could be considered. It would not be easy for White to win on the Q-side, but he would also have good chances on the K-side.

26	PxP	RxP

Karpov must have completely overlooked White's simple 27th move which both defends and pins!

27	Q-B1!	R-N2
28	B-R6	R(B1)-N1
29	BxR	RxB
30	R-R3	P-KR3
31	R(R3)-B3	N-N4
32	R-B8ch	K-R2
33	R(B2)-B6	P-B3
34	K-N2	Q-KB2
35	Q-B2	P-QR4
36	P-KN4	PxP
37	BPxP	P-R5
38	R-QR8	N-R2
39	R-R6	Q-K2
40	RxRP	R-B2
41	Q-N3	N-B3
42	R-R1	N-N5
43	R-QB1	R-B5
44	R-QN8	RxR
45	BxR	Q-QB2
46	RxN	QxB
47	Q-Q3	P-R4
48	R-N6	B-R3
49	PxP	Q-N4ch
50	Q-N3	Q-Q7ch

Black resigns

A weak performance by the world champion. He had the next game postponed.

GAME TWELVE
15th August

Looking fresh after their rest the players tried a new variation of the Ruy. New in the match, that is. The variation has been studied quite a lot in the last 30 years, and most experts give White a slight plus. This, together with the fact that Korchnoi has played it several times before, made his choice quite risky, and he did have some difficulties after the exchange of queens. But with a pawn sacrifice he got counterplay, and Karpov probably never had enough to win. At adjournment a draw was the obvious result, and it came about after some curious happenings.

Karpov offered a draw just before the session ended, but Korchnoi just made an angry gesture with his hand. He had stated repeatedly that he would consider any verbal draw offer a disturbance. When he sealed his move Karpov had left the hall. Korchnoi said something to Lothar Schmid, which was meant to be a protest against Karpov's draw offer, but Schmid misunderstood and thought that Korchnoi was ready to accept the draw.

When later it became clear that Schmid had misunderstood Korchnoi, he displayed his irresistible charm, explaining to the journalists: You see, his language is Russian, not English, and my language is German, not English, so.....

Anyway, Schmid knew as well as the players that there was no reason to play on. It seems there were some contacts at ambassadorial level between the two teams, and somehow the draw became a draw.

White: Karpov
Black: Korchnoi

Ruy Lopez

1	P-K4	P-K4
2	N-KB3	N-QB3
3	B-N5	P-QR3
4	B-R4	N-B3
5	0-0	NxP
6	P-Q4	P-QN4
7	B-N3	P-Q4
8	PxP	B-K3
9	Q-K2	

Twice P-B3 (which used to be Karpov's move in this position), twice QN-Q2 and only now the Keres or Moscow Variation. Judging by this game Korchnoi has nothing new here. He goes directly into a slightly inferior ending, convinced that a young man like Karpov cannot beat an experienced grandmaster like himself in that type of position.

9	...	B-K2
10	R-Q1	0-0
11	P-B4	NPxP

12 BxP   B-QB4

Somehow an emergency solution. Black wants to get his queen away from the Q-file. The Swedish master Folke Ekström's 12...Q-Q2, which I recommended (and played against Geller) in 1966, is bolder. However, it became so popular that a lot of theory developed.

13	B-K3	BxB
14	QxB	Q-N1
15	B-N3	N-R4

15...Q-N3 has also been played, by Korchnoi among others..The text was used by Euwe against Keres in the 1948 world championship tournament; White got a clear positional advantage after 16 QN-Q2 NxN? 17 RxN NxB 18 PxN, but the right move is 16...Q-R2!

16 N-K1!?   Q-N3!

16...NxB?17 PxN Q-N3 18 QxQ PxQ 19 P-QN4 gave White clear superiority in Hübner-Demarre, Dresden 1969. The text move is not difficult to find and certainly an improvement. Postponing NxB Black keeps the retreat square QB4 for his knight.

17	QxQ	PxQ
18	P-B3	NxB
19	RPxN	N-B4
20	P-QN4	N-Q2
21	N-Q3	P-KN4!?

Prevents both N-B4 and P-B4, but weakens the black position.

22	N-B3	KR-B1
23	N-B2	

23 ...   P-Q5!

Curiously enough 24 RxQP NxP (25 N-Q5 N-B3) is much better for Black than 23...NxP 24 NxP.

24	N-K2	P-Q6
25	NxP	B-B5

73

26	N-N3	BxN
27	RxB	NxP
28	R-Q5	N-N3!

28...P-B3 29 N-K4 loses a pawn in much worse circumstances.

29	RxNP	R-B7

Karpov's continuation is very natural and straight-forward, and it doesn't win. So the annotator tries to find a win with the "clever" move 30 R-N1. The cleverness partly consists in a later R-QR1, when KN2 is defended by the other rook and the position of the black king is open to attacks from the side. I feel quite clever, but I cannot prove a win. The idea is something like 30 R-N1 R-Q1 31 N-B5 R(Q1)-Q7 32 P-R4 K-B1 33 R-R1!, but Black defends better with 30...P-B3 31 R-N4 R-Q1 32 P-R4 K-B2.

30	P-N3	R-N7
31	N-B5	RxQNP
32	P-R4	K-B1
33	P-R5	N-K2
34	NxN	KxN
35	R-K1ch	K-B1
36	R-K4	

Or 36 P-R6 RxNP 37 R-N7 R-KR5 38 RxRP K-N1 and draws.

36	...	P-R4
37	R(K4)-N4	K-K2
38	PxP	RxRP
39	P-R6	RxR
40	RxR	P-N4
41	R-N7	R-N8ch
42	K-R2	R-Q8
43	RxRP	R-Q1
44	R-N7	**Drawn**

After 44...R-KR1 there is no reason to play on. A rather correct game, with good defence by Black in a difficult position (moves 21-28).

GAME THIRTEEN
17th and 20th August

In the Tartakower (Bondarevsky-Makogonov) Variation Korchnoi again stays away from an exact copy of his excellent seventh match game against Spassky - but his strategy is in fact very similar. The move ...P-QN3 has created a weakness in the black pawn structure, and with time and patience it should be possible to exploit it.

The game gets exciting when Karpov weakens his K-side in a quest for active counterplay. The situation reminds you of game nine. Only there it was move 33, and it was on the Q-side. Here it is a move earlier, and on the other flank. But Korchnoi's problems with the chess clock are the same. When move 40 has been made the experts praise the challenger's play, and all non-Soviet news agencies are optimistic on his behalf.

Next day the continuation of the game is postponed, at Korchnoi's request! Why? Has he sealed a move which allows an immediate draw? In that case it could be fun to keep Karpov and his group working for almost three days, and maybe Karpov would play as peacefully in game 14 as he did in game 6. Or is the position a sure win, and does he want Karpov to oscillate between hope and despair for three days?

At Centelles, in Northern Spain, we analyze like chess fans in thousands of other places all over the world. It is not quite clear, we begin to see defences for Black. Still difficult, but perhaps not lost. From the tournament in Montilla we hear that Spassky and other participants have reached similar conclusions.

Saturday the 19th, game 14 is played. Sunday the 20th, game 13 is finally finished. A shocking finish. It is a good guess that Korchnoi could never have lost this game if it had been played out before the start of game 14 ..... These two games form a pair, a pair that completely changed the match. Up to this point you might give Korchnoi a good chance, and Karpov was certainly not playing his best chess, though the Spanish duel was beginning to go in his favour. With Black he had difficulties, but, if the Ruy got knocked out, Korchnoi could still turn to his solid French Defence, especially so since he seemed able to draw slightly inferior endings.

Games 13 and 14 made a mess of all these speculations, and probably of Korchnoi's nerves too.

| White: Korchnoi | | 7 | R-B1 | P-QN3 |
| Black: Karpov | | 8 | BxN | |

Queen's Gambit Declined

8 P-K3 B-N2 9 BxN BxB 10 PxP PxP 11 P-QN4!? would have transposed into Korchnoi's seventh game against Spassky and, without any doubt, into the result of many hours of analysis by Karpov's team.

1	P-QB4	N-KB3
2	N-QB3	P-K3
3	N-B3	P-Q4
4	P-Q4	B-K2
5	B-N5	P-KR3
6	B-R4	0-0

8 ...   BxB

9	PxP	PxP
10	P-KN3!?	

A little different, but basically the same. The position of the white bishop does not matter much, except that on KN2 it will be very well placed if Black tries an early …P-QB4, weakening his QP.

10	…	P-B3
11	B-N2	B-B4
12	0-0	Q-Q3
13	P-K3	N-Q2

If Black's QNP could go back to its original square, he would have a very strong position. As it is, White's plans include P-QN4(-N5) and also in some cases P-K4, to attack the weak black pawns.

14	N-K1	KR-K1
15	N-Q3	P-N3
16	N-B4	B-N2

16…P-KR4 and 16…B-N4 came into consideration.

17	P-KN4!	B-K3
18	P-KR3	N-B1
19	NxB	NxN

Why does White exchange Black's

"bad" bishop? Again: because the black QN-pawn is not on its original square! This bishop could have been important for the defence of QB3 and Q4.

20	Q-Q3	QR-Q1
21	R-B2	N-B2
22	N-R4	

A clumsy-looking move, but White wants to make sure that Black does not play …P-QB4.

22	…	Q-Q2
23	P-N3	R-K3
24	N-B3	R-Q3(?)

Not 24…P-QB4? 25 PxP PxP 26 N-R4. But 24…B-B1 must be more exact, for instance 25 N-K2 B-Q3 26 KR-B1 N-K1, with the plan …B-N1 followed by …N-N2 and …P-KR4.

25	P-N4	B-B1
26	N-K2	P-QN4!?

A drastic solution. Probably not the best move, but the idea may be to bring the game to a crisis before the time control at move forty!

Against patient black defence, White would patiently make progress: double rooks on the QB-file, and play P-QR4, threatening P-QN5 all the time.

| 27 | Q-N3 | N-R1 |
| 28 | P-QR4 | PxP!? |

The same tactics. After 28...P-R3 29 P-R5 White would bring his knight to Q3 and get past the time control with his positional advantage intact.

29	QxRP	N-N3
30	Q-N3	R-N1
31	N-B4	N-B5
32	Q-R4	P-KB4?!

Positionally unsound, but something has to be done before move 40. The threat was R-R1 followed by B-B1.

33	PxP	QxP
34	QxRP!	RxP
35	R-R2	Q-B1
36	R-B1	R-N2
37	Q-R4?	

Simpler, better and wiser 37 Q-R8! (37...R-N1 38 Q-R6). An exchange of queens would offer White good winning chances. The dark-squared black bishop is not a good defender for the weak white-squared QBP.

| 37 | ... | R-KB2! |

Threatening strong counterplay with ...RxN.

| 38 | RxN!? | PxR |

Not 38...RxN? because of 39 RxP!

| 39 | QxP(B4) | Q-B4 |
| 40 | N-Q3(?) | |

40! Of course not 40 BxP?? RxB 41 QxR(B6) Q-N8ch, but 40 R-R8! was stronger. The knight leaves a good square.

| 40 | ... | B-N2(?) |

Safer 40...Q-QN4.

A difficult position to analyze. Of course White can get the black QB-pawn, after which he has two strong pawns for the exchange and can never lose (sic!). But how does he win? Or get winning chances? Not with 41 N-N4 P-B4, for example 42 QxP QxQ 43 PxQ R-Q8ch 44 K-R2 B-K4ch 45 P-B4 RxP!

Korchnoi spent 40 minutes on his sealed move. As Stean says, you cannot keep him out of time trouble.

If you like chronological order, you may now turn to game 14!

On August 20th there followed:

41 R-R7

The move most experts expected. 41...Q-K3 42 QxQ RxQ 43 R-R6 is difficult for Black (43...R-B2?? 44 B-Q5!)

41 ... R-B3!
42 RxR

42 N-K5 QxBPch 43 K-R1 Q-K8ch! 44 K-R2 QxP 45 NxR Q-B5ch is a dead draw.
42 R-N7!?, stopping 42...Q-QN4 and even 42...K-R2 (because of 43 P-K4!), is a tricky continuation. But Black can play 42...B-B1.

42 ... RxR
43 P-Q5

Probably trying to surprise Black. 43 BxP K-R2 looks like the normal continuation, and Black ought to hold the game.

43 ... B-K4
44 PxP K-N2

45 B-K4

Playing with fire. NxB offered no

real winning chances, but White could never lose.

What did Korchnoi's seconds find? And an even better question: what would he have played, if he had drawn game 14?

45 ... Q-N4ch
46 K-B1 B-Q3
47 B-Q5 R-K2
48 B-B3(?)

Already very strange. 48 B-K6 looks good, on Q7 the bishop would defend the KR-pawn.

48 ... P-R4
49 B-Q1

This must be a very deep move.

49 ... Q-KB4
50 K-K2 R-K5
51 Q-B3ch Q-B3
52 Q-N3 Q-B4

Is Karpov playing for a win already? And why does Korchnoi, in his usual desperate time pressure, not repeat the position?

53 Q-N7ch R-K2
54 Q-N2ch K-R2
55 Q-Q4 B-B2

56 Q-KR4???

It makes no sense to spend 40 minutes on move 41 and make such a blunder on the last move before the next time control. 56 P-R4 and several others would probably have lead to a draw.

56 ... R-K5

The queen has no square.

57	P-B4	B-N3
58	B-B2	RxKPch
59	K-Q2	Q-R4ch
60	K-Q1	Q-R8ch
61	K-Q2	R-K5
	Resigns	

The terrible thing about chess is that you only have yourself to blame.

Smyslov
1957-1958

Tal
1960-1961

79

With game 13 still adjourned, the Spanish duel continues. We all know now that Korchnoi ought to have been less stubborn. Why not the French? At least this is the easiest story to tell; Korchnoi went on playing the Open Ruy until the Soviet analysts found a hole in his preparations. This was demonstrated in the very important and decisive game fourteen.

But this is not the whole truth. The opening resulted in a slightly uncomfortable ending, but probably Black could still hold the position. The decisive factor in this game was that for once Korchnoi failed to outplay Karpov in the ending. It is fair to say that he outplayed himself, though some very good play by Karpov helped. If you want to enter into really wild speculation, how about this theory: Karpov's victory in this game was due to his weak endgame play in games ten and twelve! It may sound crazy, but look at Korchnoi's rook manoeuvre on moves 27-28. He plays as if he is sure that nothing can happen to him. This is very far from his usual tough and resourceful defence in difficult positions.

White: Karpov
Black: Korchnoi

Ruy Lopez

1	P-K4	P-K4
2	N-KB3	N-QB3
3	B-N5	P-QR3
4	B-R4	N-B3
5	0-0	NxP
6	P-Q4	P-QN4
7	B-N3	P-Q4
8	PxP	B-K3
9	P-B3	B-QB4

As in games 2 and 4.

10	QN-Q2	0-0
11	B-B2	B-B4

In his youth Korchnoi is reported to have played quite a lot of poker, much to the dislike of the officials in the Soviet Chess Federation. You may say that he still plays that game. Here he wante to "see". Is Karpov bluffing?

12	N-N3	B-KN5

13 P-KR3!?

Does this kill the variation? Maybe, but not because it gives many winning chances. The trouble is that Black gets an absolutely unattractive position.

13...BxN 14 PxB BxPch 15 RxB NxR 16 KxN NxP 17 B-K3 or B-KB4 must be good for White. Black's QB4 is a hole in his pawn structure which will make it difficult for him to get the Q-side pawn majority moving, and White's pieces will soon be ready to attack.

13	...	B-R4
14	P-N4	B-KN3

"The position is unclear", says the *Encyclopaedia of Chess Openings*. The chapter is by Korchnoi. How much did he analyze when he wrote this more than four years ago?

15	BxN	PxB
16	NxB	PxN
17	B-B4	QxQ

There is nothing else. Black cannot exploit the weakness of the white king's position. The white knight on B5 is very strong, and 17...Q-K2 is refuted by 18 Q-Q5.

18	QRxQ	N-Q1!

He cannot allow the white knight to stay in its dominating position.

19	R-Q7	N-K3
20	NxN	PxN
21	B-K3	QR-B1!

The plausible 21...R-B2 is much weaker. After 22 KR-Q1 QR-KB1 comes B-B5!

22	KR-Q1	B-K5
23	B-B5	KR-K1

The black defence has many successes to show. The strong white knight was eliminated, the rook will be kicked away from the seventh, and the advanced KBP is protected. But still White has the initiative, and Black has very little active play. Who wants to play this opening variation with Black now?

24	R(Q7)-Q4	B-Q4(?)

Not a very serious error, but not very exact either. 24...B-B3 was better, for instance 25 P-KR4 P-QR4 when White's best is 26 P-N3. After 26 K-R2 P-R5 27 K-N3 B-Q4 all Black's problems would be solved. Against 26 P-N3 Black plays 26...R-R1 followed by ...P-R5. The point is that with Black's bishop on Q4 White counters ...P-R5 with P-QB4.

It is quite possible that Korchnoi had his plan ready here, the losing plan.

25	P-N3	P-QR4

All this cost Karpov 20 minutes against Korchnoi's 84. Karpov's quick play may have had some effect on the challenger, though he ought to be too old and experienced for that.

And even he had more than an hour for the next 15 moves.

26 K-R2   R-R1
27 K-N3

27 ...   R-R3?

27...P-R5 or 27...B-B3 would have been natural. The latter seems best. Against 27...P-R5 White plays 28 P-B4 NPxP 29 PxBP B-B3 30 P-R3. He can then block the QN-file with B-N4 and proceed with his plans on the K-side. They begin with P-KR4-R5. If Black does nothing, White plays P-N5, threatening P-N6 followed by R-B4-B7. If Black avoids this by ...P-N3, White switches both rooks to the KR-file. Black must play ...P-R3 early to avoid all these difficulties. White then plays K-R4 and P-N5, and after the exchange of pawns his king goes back to KR4. The black king probably stands on KR2, (otherwise the white attack on the KN-file will be strong), and at an opportune moment White plays R-KB4 QR-Q1; R-KN1 R-Q2; R-N6 followed by K-N5, B-B8 and P-R6. I do not guarantee that all this is possible against best defence, but at least this plan of attack shows that White has something in the position.

But back to Black's 27th move. Korchnoi's real mistake is that he does not admit the slight error on move 24. 27...B-B3! prepares ...P-R5. After 28 P-KR4 P-R5 29 P-N4 B-Q4 30 P-R3 QR-N1 followed by ...R-N2, ...P-B3 and ...R-KB2 Black has no more problems. (28 P-KR4 P-R5) 29 PxP RxP also brings the draw within reach. White would probably try 28 P-B4 PxP 29 PxP QR-N1 30 B-R3, but this is very different from the other line (with B-N4 and P-R3) for two reasons: the QN-file is not blocked, and the black bishop has the square QR5. There might follow 30...P-R3 31 P-R4 B-R5, and after any rook move the bishop returns to B3, preparing ...R-Q1 or ...R-N8 (maybe ...K-R2 first).

So, in my opinion the black position is tenable with 27...B-B3! The opening did not lose, the inaccuracy on move 24 did not lose. It is not quite sure that 27...R-R3? loses, but it prepares the losing move.

28 P-KR4   R-B3?

It is difficult to imagine Black playing the rook back to R1, and the white attack with 29 P-R5 etc. may already be too strong. But what did

Korchnoi think when he played the rook move? White's reply is virtually forced. Did Black overlook move 33?

29	RxB!	PxR
30	RxP	R(B3)-K3
31	B-Q4	P-B3
32	R-B5	

32 ...   R-KB1(?)

A much better try was 32...R-Q1 33 KxP R-Q4 34 RxR PxR. This in accordance with a general rule: if you are an exchange up, exchange your opponent's last rook.

My comments, claiming Black's 28th move to be the losing mistake, required a lot of analysis of this ending after 34...PxR. White has two

strong pawns for the exchange, but to begin with I found sufficient counter-play for Black after 35 K-K3? R-KR3 36 P-R5 P-N3!, and also after 35 K-N3 P-N5. 35 K-K2 was no improvement because of the answer 35...P-R4! (with advantage for Black!). Correct is 35 P-R3 or 35 P-R5. The safest line is 35 P-R3 P-N3 36 P-R5! (but not 36 K-N3? P-R4!) 36...K-B2 37 K-B4. By exact play this seems to win; the white pawns become too strong.

33 P-R4!

White wins pawn number two for the exchange, with an overwhelming position.

33	...	PxP
34	PxP	P-N3

Or 34...R-R1 35 KxP followed by K-K4 and P-KB4.

35	RxRP	R(K3)-K1
36	R-R7	R-B2
37	R-R6!	

You see? The exchange down, White is not interested in giving up his last rook (37 RxR? KxR 38 P-QR5 K-K3 followed by ...K-Q4 and ...P-B4).

37	...	R-B2

37...R-QB1 looks better, but 38 P-QR5 P-B4 39 P-K6 is more than convincing.

38	B-B5!	R(B2-B1)

38...RxP 39 B-Q6 is pure beauty.

39	B-Q6	R-R1
40	RxP	RxRP
41	KxP	P-R4

Adjourned. But no doubt about the result. The continuation was played after the shocking finale of game 13.

42	PxP	PxP
43	P-B4	R-R7
44	R-N6	

Wins with the QB-pawn. After 44 K-K3 he would win with the KB-pawn, but it would require more exact play because Black would take the KR-pawn.

44	...	K-B2
45	P-B5	R-R5
46	P-B6	K-K3
47	P-B7	K-Q2
48	R-N8	R-QB1
49	K-K3	RxRP

White was ready to advance the KBP.

50	P-K6ch!	Resigns

Because of 50...KxP 51 B-N3! Equally hopeless is 50...KxB 51 RxR R-QB5 52 R-Q8ch KxBP 53 R-Q7ch K-B3 54 P-B4.

To some experts it came as a surprise that Korchnoi did not postpone this game. But when it was played the outcome was as expected. Korchnoi probably too shaken to play for a win, Karpov probably happy to "consolidate" his two point lead.

But in spite of everything it was not an uninteresting game; the first Catalan in the match, a sharp pawn sacrifice by Black, some interesting complications. It is worth noting that on move 16 Korchnoi did not go in for a combination which would have lead to a draw at once.

White: Korchnoi
Black: Karpov

Catalan Opening

1	P-QB4	N-KB3
2	N-QB3	P-K3
3	N-B3	P-Q4
4	P-Q4	B-K2
5	P-KN3	0-0
6	B-N2	PxP
7	N-K5	N-B3!?

7...P-B4 used to be routine here, but the sharp knight move has been played by several masters during the last few years. Petrosian used it in one game in his 1977 match against Korchnoi and drew more easily than with P-B4.

8	BxN	PxB

9	NxP(B6)	Q-K1
10	NxBch	QxN
11	Q-R4	P-B4!
12	QxBP	PxP
13	QxQP	P-K4

White is a pawn up, but Black has two kinds of compensation. A slight lead in development and attacking chances against the white K-side where the fianchetto bishop is sadly missing.

Against Korchnoi you shouldn't sacrifice pawns for nothing. He takes them! So this variation must have been studied carefully in Karpov's camp. A continuation like 14 Q-QR4 Q-N2 15 P-K4 B-R6 looks very unpleasant for White.

14	Q-KR4	R-N1!

A nice multi-purpose move. The critical continuation is 15 0-0 R-N5 16 P-K4 Q-N2 17 R-K1 or P-B3, Korchnoi might have gone into this if he had been either in top form or desperate; he was neither.

15	B-N5!?	RxP
16	0-0	

The immediate draw is 16 N-Q5 Q-N2 17 NxNch PxN 18 0-0 PxB 19 QxNPch with perpetual check.

16	...	Q-K3
17	BxN	QxB
18	QxQ	PxQ
19	QR-N1	RxR
20	RxR	B-K3

A strong bishop for Black, the better pawn structure for White. The position is even, and with very little play left. 21 R-N7 R-B1 22 N-K4 K-N2 23 RxRP R-B7 can only be dangerous for White.

21	P-B3	R-B1
22	R-QB1	R-N1
23	R-B2	R-QB1
24	K-B2	BxP
25	RxB	Drawn

Korchnoi's English seconds, Raymond Keene and Michael Stean, did their best, on many occasions during the match, to keep the psychological warfare within reasonable limits. When Petra Leeuwerik complained about the signals, between the Russian seconds and Karpov, which could possibly be hidden in their choice of which yoghourt to send up to him, Keene wrote a very funny letter to Lothar Schmid; its content ought to have made it perfectly clear that the complaint was not serious. But, formally, it was still a written protest, and Schmid felt he had to take it seriously. Petra took it seriously. Baturinsky took it seriously. So the yoghourt question kept officials and journalists busy for a couple of days. In the end, Karpov could have blueberry yoghourt at 7.15 p.m., while other flavours needed a written request from him to the arbiters.

But Keene likes to tease Baturinsky! There was an earth tremor the night after game fourteen. Keene was asked about it the next day. Had he been nervous? Oh no, not at all; he had not realised that the earth was shaking, he had thought that it was just Baturinsky falling down the stairs!

When Karpov refused to shake hands with Korchnoi, because of the latter's continued verbal attacks on Dr Zoukhar, Keene made a remark about Korchnoi not needing to wash his hands. This made Baturinsky very angry and Keene tried in vain to placate him with a nice present of a monogrammed cigar.

GAME SIXTEEN
24th August

A typhoon struck the Philippines. In Baguio it killed two people and caused much damage. There was no light in the playing hall, and there were some problems with the roof. The organizers wanted to postpone the game, but the players did not. A team of electricians got to work, and it was possible to start at the normal time. The show must go on.

Not unexpectedly Korchnoi gave up the Ruy in this game, to return to the French which drew every time against Karpov in 1974. Both players obviously wanted to try a well-known ending with an isolated black queen's pawn. White must have a small advantage, but Korchnoi wants to prove something. Either that the position is tenable, or that Karpov cannot beat him in such endings. If the result of one game is proof, he proved it.

Around move 27 a draw offer would have been understandable. Perhaps the players did not want to go out into the rain. Or maybe they were still full of aggression after the discussion about the chairs. The Russian delegation had discovered that Korchnoi enjoyed an unjust psychological advantage because he could look down upon Karpov. They wanted the seats of the two chairs to be at exactly the same altitude, 50 centimetres above floor level. The logic of this escapes me, and it could very well be argued that the handicap is on the other side because the air is thinner up where Korchnoi breathes. Petra Leeuwerik was quoted for a rather angry remark; she suggested that the Russians might like to remove Korchnoi's head so that the two players would be of the same height.

All manufacturers of chairs for chess matches will no doubt follow this important discussion with great interest.

White: Karpov
Black: Korchnoi

French Defence

1	P-K4	P-K3
2	P-Q4	P-Q4
3	N-Q2	P-QB4
4	KPxP	KPxP
5	B-N5ch	B-Q2

5...N-B3 is more complicated, ambitious, risky etcetera.

6	Q-K2ch	Q-K2
7	BxBch	NxB
8	PxP	NxP
9	N-N3	QxQch
10	NxQ	NxN
11	RPxN	B-B4

12	B-Q2	N-K2

In my opinion, White has a clear advantage! Small, but very clear. I don't like isolated pawns. And I also believe that 13 B-B3 (Botvinnik-Euwe

1948) must be the right move.

(On this same day the round in the Spanish team championship was delayed more than four hours; a thunderstorm caused a power failure. When we finally got started I accepted an isolated QP against Pomar, with White in a Panov Attack. I won in 23 moves! My queen did wonderful things. The point is that Korchnoi has no queen.)

13 N-B4

Karpov has prepared this move together with several leading experts, so I cannot bring myself to put a question mark. Also, there is such a thing as psychology, and surprise value and all that.

13	...	0-0
14	0-0	KR-Q1
15	N-Q3	B-N3
16	P-B3	P-B3
17	KR-Q1	K-B2
18	K-B1	N-B4
19	B-K1	N-K2

Surprising, but not so bad. What is the white bishop doing on K1?

20	N-N4	R-Q2
21	R-Q3	QR-Q1

22	QR-Q1	K-K3

The weak pawn gets some over-protection. The black position looks okay even to me.

23	B-Q2	N-B3
24	NxN	PxN

Instead of the QP it is now the QRP which is isolated and weak. But the white pawn structure also contains a slight weakness, the doubled pawn.

25	P-QN4	K-B2
26	B-K3	BxB
27	RxB	R-QN1
28	R-K2	R-N4
29	R-R1	R(Q2)-N2

Toying with the possibilities ...P-QR4 and ...P-QB4.

30	R-Q2	K-K3
31	R-R6	R(N4)-N3
32	R-R2	K-Q3
33	K-K2	R-K2ch
34	K-Q3	P-QR3
35	R-Q1	K-B2

Planning 36 R(Q1)-QR1 K-N2. White's position still looks prefer-able, but it is difficult to find a con-structive plan.

36	R(R2)-R1	K-Q1
37	P-B3	R-K4!

The strong position of this rook compensates for the slightly inferior pawn structure.

38	K-Q4	K-B2

38...R-K7 39 R-K1 RxKNP 40 K-B5 is too dangerous.

39	R-K1	K-Q3
40	P-KB4(?)	

Good enough, but P-R4 seems more exact, to have less pawns en prise on the second row. Some experts said that Karpov ought to have spent more time on the ending.

40	...	RxR
41	RxR	P-QR4!
42	PxP	Drawn

The game was adjourned, Korchnoi probably sealing 42...RxP. After some analysis a meeting between Keene and Balashov made it unnecessary to continue. After 43 R-QR1 P-QB4ch 44 K-K3 K-B2 45 P-R6 K-N1 46 R-R5 RxP 47 P-R7ch K-R1 48 RxP RxP 49 RxP the position is rather boring.

GAME SEVENTEEN
26th August

If this game does not teach Korchnoi to stay out of time trouble, he will never learn. He lost a position it seemed impossible to lose. What is the use of absorbing all the little details of the position at move thirteen, what is the use of all your brilliant planning around move 26, if you overlook a mate in three on move 39?

The history of title matches is full of blunders. The nervous tension, and fatigue late in the matches, produce an atmosphere in which the players make more serious errors than in normal tournament chess. This game will be remembered for its last move, not for all the interesting ideas in opening and middle game. Korchnoi came close to winning it, which would have meant 2-3 instead of 1-4.

White: Korchnoi
Black: Karpov

Nimzo-Indian Defence

1	P-QB4	N-KB3
2	N-QB3	P-K3
3	P-Q4	B-N5
4	P-K3	0-0
5	B-Q3	P-B4
6	P-Q5?!	P-QN4?!
7	QPxP	BPxP
8	PxP	P-QR3

In game seven Black played 8...B-N2 and White answered 9 N-B3. It is not clear that the text is an improvement. It is quite nice for White to have his knight on K2 where it is not molested by the advance of the black KP and White is ready for the counter P-KB4.

9	N-K2	P-Q4
10	0-0	P-K4
11	P-QR3	PxP
12	BxNP	

| 12 | ... | BxN |

After 12...B-R4 13 P-QN4! or 12...P-B5 13 P-K4!, Black has no compensation for the pawn.

13 PxB!?

13 NxB was not bad, but Black would keep an impressive centre.

Now White's QN-pawn is promoted to the rank of centre pawn.

13	...	B-R3
14	R-N1	Q-Q3
15	P-QB4	P-Q5
16	N-N3	N-B3
17	P-QR4	N-QR4
18	Q-Q3	Q-K3
19	PxP	BPxP

After 19...KPxP 20 B-R3, White would have a clear advantage.

20	P-B5	KR-B1
21	P-B4!	

21 B-R3 has been suggested but is much weaker. Black does not play 21...N-B5? 22 B-N4, but 21...N-Q4! 22 N-K4 N-KB5 with good chances.

21	...	RxP
22	BxB	QxB
23	QxQ	RxQ
24	B-R3	R-Q4
25	N-B5	K-B2
26	PxP	RxP

Korchnoi was already short of time. Would it not have been simpler to play 27 NxQP.? If then 27...N-B5 28 R-N7ch gives White good chances in all continuations, e.g. 28...K-N1

29 B-K7 or 28...K-N3 29 B-B8 or 28...K-K1 29 B-B1.

Black's best defence to 27 NxQP is probably 27...K-N3, and if there is nothing else for White, he can play 28 R-R1 and try to save the QR-pawn. In many cases it will be possible to attack on the K-side later.

With so few pawns left Black would have drawing chances, but that is the same as to say that White would have winning chances.

27	R-N5?!	N-B5!
28	R-N7ch	K-K3
29	NxQPch	

Understandable. After 29 NxNPch K-Q4, Black would be very well centralized.

29	...	K-Q4
30	N-B3	NxB

31 NxR

After 31 R-Q1ch K-K3 32 N-Q4ch! K-Q4 33 N-N5ch K-B3 34 R-QB7ch K-N3 35 R-Q6ch K-R4 36 RxRch KxR 37 NxN, White would have winning chances. But after 31...K-B3! 32 R-N3 R-K5 33 RxN R(R3)xP 34 R-B3ch K-N3, Black draws without much difficulty, even though his king is on the wrong side of the board.

31	...	KxN
32	R-K7ch	K-Q5
33	RxP?	

It was more logical to chase the black king further away from the K-side by 33 R-Q1ch!, followed by 34 R-QB7ch and then 35 RxP. By exact play Black can probably draw, but it would not be easy.

| 33 | ... | N-B5 |
| 34 | R-B4ch | |

Still playing for a win. Of course, 34 R-KB7 K-K4 35 R-K7ch was an easy draw.

| 34 | ... | N-K5 |
| 35 | R-Q7ch? | |

35 RxP was best, but offers no real winning chances.

35	...	K-K6
36	R-B3ch	K-K7
37	RxP	N(B5)-Q7

| 38 | R-QR3(?) | R-QB3 |

39 R-R1??

39 P-N4! still draws easily, but not 39 P-R4?? R-B8ch 40 K-R2 N-B8ch 41 K-R3 N-B7 mate.

| 39 | ... | N-KB6ch! |
| | **Resigns** | |

Because of 40 PxN R-KN3ch and mate next move.

Journalists had trouble digging up stories on free days, but Keene and Stean were often very helpful (while some gentlemen of the press complained about the difficulty of communicating with the Russian delegation), for instance Stean gave one journalist a wonderful story about the reasons for Korchnoi's lack of concentration. The owl had died! A Philippine baby owl, named Viktor, had been adopted by Korchnoi, who had come to feel very close to it, but it died. The marvellous thing about such stories is that it does not really matter whether they are true. The main point is to keep the journalists and their readers happy, and keep chess in the news even when there is no chess to write about. (In Reykjavik, in 1972, a chess master told his newspaper that if they wanted daily reports about the colour of Spassky's trousers, they had to find a new chess correspondent. It is sometimes difficult for chess masters to get used to modern journalism. In the good old days, would it have been news that Dr Zoukhar tried to buy a book about the famous Philippine faith healers?).

GAME EIGHTEEN
2nd and 3rd September

After the shock in game seventeen Korchnoi wanted a pause and postponed game eighteen twice. He held a press conference, blaming the organizers for this and that, then he fired Petra Leeuwerik. According to some of the wire services Keene was then made chief of the delegation, but the next day another announcement said it was Stean. In any case, the trend seemed to be away from the very serious anti-Soviet statements towards the less serious anti-Baturinsky jokes. Instead of trying to beat the government of a super power Korchnoi should just try to beat Karpcv. But how?

After giving up the Ruy Lopez he had turned to his trusted French Defence in game sixteen, but the result could only be called satisfactory if you were very, very modest. What else was there? Sicilian? Alekhine? Pirc? He has played them all. Maybe the Pirc was chosen because of two Karpov games from 1977 in which the champion came close to defeat.

Karpov deviated from those games as early as move 8. It was one of those novelties which is not important for theory but may be useful in a match. It did not really change the character of the position, but various calculations had to be made over the board instead of being copied from known games or home analysis.

On moves 17 and 19 improvements may be found for Black, who got a difficult ending with an isolated pawn. Karpov lost most of his advantage before the adjournment, and later his winning attempts led to nothing. When he finally offered a draw he did so directly, not via the arbiter. Korchnoi did not answer directly, but he did not protest either - he just signed the score sheets.

White: Karpov
Black: Korchnoi

Pirc Defence

1	P-K4	P-Q3
2	P-Q4	N-KB3
3	N-QB3	P-KN3

It was Pirc who made this opening popular in international tournaments. Hence the names Pirc Defence and Yugoslav Defence. But at that time there was political tension between Stalin and Tito, so the Russians gave the opening the name of a master who had played it during the 1930s - Ufimtsev. In Hungary a certain Antal had written about it - you may now guess what it is called among the sons of the Puzta.

It was much nicer in the good old days when it was just called irregular, though this was not for lack of names. Great masters such as Paulsen, Charousek and Pillsbury played this irregular opening, Paulsen even played it very well sometimes. In Nurnberg 1896 Charousek played this defence against Tarrasch and got murdered. He then turned to Steinitz and asked what he had done wrong. The ex-champion had played many strange openings in his day, but showed no understanding for this one: "Young man, when you play such a bizarre opening you should not be surprised if you lose".

4	N-B3	B-N2
5	B-K2	0-0

6	0-0	B-N5
7	B-K3	N-B3

8   Q-Q3!?

Not in the books, but reliable Pirc fans tell me that it has been played before. More common are 8 Q-Q2, 8 P-Q5 and 8 R-K1.

Karpov-Adorjan, Las Palmas 1977, went 8 Q-Q2 P-K4 9 P-Q5 N-K2 10 QR-Q1 B-Q2 11 N-K1 N-N5 12 BxN BxB 13 P-B3 B-Q2 14 P-B4 B-N5 15 R-N1 P-QB3 16 P-KR3 B-Q2 17 QPxP? BxBP 18 R-Q1 PxP 19 RxP P-B4, and Black had the initiative. The improvement 17 BPxP QPxP 18 P-Q6 (Karpov-Timman, Tilburg 1977) gave rise to an obscure position which Karpov did not handle very well.

8	...	P-K4
9	P-Q5	N-N5

It is not clear that the white queen is better placed on Q3 if Black plays 9...N-K2. Since every opening played in a title match is copied all over the world, there will probably soon be enough material for a nice theoretical article, with the usual conclusion: this needs further testing.

10	Q-Q2	P-QR4

11	P-KR3	B-Q2
12	B-KN5	Q-K1
13	N-R2	K-R1!

Provides the knight with a retreat square.

14	P-R3	N-R3
15	B-R6	BxB
16	QxB	N-KN1
17	Q-K3	

17   ...   P-KB4

Probably a temperamental decision. The alternative was 17...P-R5 18 P-B4 PxP 19 RxP N-B4 20 QR-KB1 P-KB3, with a solid but passive position.

18	PxP	BxP
19	QR-B1	N-B3?

There were many other possibilities, of which two or three were probably preferable. 19...N-B4 was probably rejected because of 20 P-P-QN4 (20...PxP 21 PxP N-R5 is not quite clear as 22 N-N5 might cause problems). 19...P-R5 was quite possible, as were 19...B-Q2 and 19...Q-K2, which latter move looks best to this commentator. With the black-squared bishop gone and the king on a black square, the queen ought to defend some squares of that colour.

20	P-KN4	B-Q2
21	P-B4	PxP
22	QxP	N-B4
23	QR-K1	N(B3)-K5

A difficult choice between this and 23...Q-K4 24 QxQ PxQ, when White should probably continue quietly with a move like 25 N-B3. As in the game, after move 27, the isolated black pawn is weak, but attempts to win it quickly give Black counterchances. For example 25 P-N5 N-R4 26 RxRch RxR 27 BxN PxB 28 K-N2 B-B4, or 27 B-N4 N-B5.

24	Q-K3	Q-K4
25	NxN	NxN
26	B-B3	N-N4
27	QxQch	PxQ
28	B-N2	RxRch
29	NxR	R-K1

Without any doubt White has the advantage, but Karpov probably loses half of it with his mext move. 30 P-N3!, to keep the pawn majority mobile, was strongest.

30	N-Q2?	P-R5!

Long live Philidor! His operas are

almost forgotten, but in the chess world he is remembered as the strongest player of the 18th century and an important thinker and writer. He understood that it was not always wrong to have your pawns on the same colour squares as the bishop. He said that this was correct on the flank where you have to defend!

There was a beautiful example of this in the second match game between Polugaevsky and Korchnoi, Evian 1977. "Polu" had four pawns against three on the Q-side, but they were on R2, N3, B4 and Q5. A nice chain? Oh no, for there were only rooks and bishops on the board and the bishops were black squared. Black's bishop stood on Q3, his pawns on QB2, QN3 and QR4. White's pawns were immobile and on the other flank Black was a pawn up.

31	R-K3	K-N2
32	K-B2(?)	

After the previous move, 32 R-QB3 R-QB1 33 K-B2 was the natural continuation.

32	...	R-K2
33	P-B4	P-N3
34	R-QB3	P-R4!

Secures some kind of counterplay

on this side. If White plays 35 PxP PxP 36 K-N3, which is probably best, at least Black gets many tactical chances with the white king in the open.

35	K-N3	PxP
36	PxP	B-K1
37	P-B5	PxP
38	N-K4	NxNch
39	BxN	K-B3
40	RxP	K-N4

Adjourned. Karpov sealed his next move.

Black has four isolated pawns, but the threats against the white KNP save him.

41	B-Q3	R-B2
42	B-K2	R-R2
43	B-B3	R-B2
44	R-B4	R-R2
45	R-N4	R-K2
46	K-B2	B-Q2
47	K-N3	B-K1
48	K-B2	B-Q2
49	K-K3	P-K5!

Otherwise White gets chances with B-Q1.

50	BxP	KxP
51	K-B2	K-N4
52	B-B2	R-K4
53	BxRP	BxB
54	RxB	RxP
55	K-K3	R-N4
56	P-N4	R-K4ch

Avoiding the trap 56...P-B4?? 57 R-R5!

57	K-Q4	K-B5
58	R-R8	P-N4
59	R-QB8	R-K5ch
60	K-Q5	R-K4ch
61	K-B6	P-N5

Instructive. Black wanted the white king to obstruct the QB-file.

62	RxP	P-N6
63	K-N6	P-N7
64	R-B1	K-B6
	Drawn	

The continuation could be 65 P-R4 R-K5, or 65...K-B7 66 P-R5 R-K8 67 R-B2ch R-K7 68 R-B1, etc.

GAME NINETEEN
7th September

Karpov had this game postponed. The majority of news stories emanating from Baguio now called Keene the head of Korchnoi's delegation, but Petra Leeuwerik was still in evidence. She threatened the organizers with all kinds of scandals when the security guards would not allow two 'gurus' to enter the playing hall. It seems that these two Americans, Stephen Dwyer and Victoria Shepperd, had been teaching Korchnoi meditation. (In my opinion chess masters ought to teach gurus meditation.) Also interesting was the fact that they were free on bail while appealing against a seventeen-year jail sentence for stabbing an Indian diplomat.

After a long discussion the gurus were allowed in. In their colourful saffron robes and sitting in the lotus position they were really more interesting to watch than the game.

White: Korchnoi
Black: Karpov

Catalan Opening

1	P-QB4	N-KB3
2	P-KN3	P-K3
3	B-N2	P-Q4
4	N-KB3	B-K2
5	P-Q4	0-0
6	QN-Q2	

Rather passive, but Korchnoi has obviously not found an improvement on game 15.

6	...	P-QN3
7	0-0	B-N2
8	PxP	

One of the Korchnoi-Petrosian match games went 8 P-N3 QN-Q2 9 B-N2 P-B4, with no problems for Black.

8	...	PxP
9	N-K5	QN-Q2
10	N(Q2)-B3	

The game to improve on is Kirov-Padevski, Bulgarian Championship 1977!: 10 N(Q2)-B4?! N-K5 11 Q-B2 NxN 12 NxN B-Q3 13 B-B4 R-K1 14 KR-Q1 Q-K2 15 N-Q3, with some advantage for White. One of the possible improvements is 10...P-B4.

10	...	P-B4
11	P-N3	

To stop ...P-B5, but the move also gives Black a target.

11	...	P-QR4!
12	B-N2	N-K5
13	R-B1	R-K1
14	NxN	QxN
15	N-K5	Q-K3
16	N-Q3	B-Q3

Threatening ...P-B5.

97

17	PxP	PxP

The hanging pawns? Karpov often accepts them; in the Queen's Gambit, Queen's Indian and other openings. Korchnoi likes to play against them. But in this position Black's pieces are very active.

Of course 18 BxN? QxB 19 NxP BxN 20 RxB P-Q5 21 P-B3 Q-K6ch, followed by ...P-Q6, is dangerous for White.

18	P-K3	P-R5
19	PxP	B-R3
20	R-K1	BxN
21	QxB	RxP
22	Q-N3	R(R5)-R1
23	BxN	

Again ...P-B5 was a threat.

23	...	PxB

Better than 23...QxB? 24 KR-Q1 P-B5 25 Q-N5, for instance 25...B-K4 26 BxB RxB 27 R-Q4 Q-B4 28 P-QR4, with chances for White. Instead of 25...B-K4, 25...RxP, with a safe draw, is better.

The text is not a very serious winning attempt by Black.

24	QxQ	RxQ

25	P-QR3	R-R5
26	KR-Q1	P-B3
27	K-B1	K-B2

Black has the more comfortable position, but hardly any winning chances.

28	R-B2	B-K2
29	R-Q7	R-N3
30	P-N4	K-K3
31	R-B7	R-R1
32	R-Q2	P-N3
33	K-N2	

But not 33 R(Q2)-Q7?? B-Q3!

33	...	P-B4
34	P-N5	R-Q3
35	R-B2	R(Q3)-R3
36	P-KR4	R(R1)-R2
37	R-B8	R-R1

The exchange of a pair of rooks would favour Black.

38	R-B7	R(R1)-R2
39	R-B8	Drawn

A correct and not very exciting game. But let me not forget to mention that the two gurus belong to an Indian sect called Ananda Marga.

The commentators looked foolish again in their newspaper columns all over the world. But was I really wrong to predict an easy victory for Karpov at the adjournment? Reports from Baguio said that Korchnoi thought he could draw. Well, he had to be optimistic: 1-5 would be too much.

In Tilburg, where a very strong Grandmaster tournament was in progress, I saw many masters analyze the adjourned position. Everybody was convinced that Karpov would win with 42 QxP. How could we know that he had found another move?

Even though he drew, it still remains a question whether the Caro-Kann with 5...KPxN is the answer to Korchnoi's problems with Black. I do not believe that this opening suits his style, and I think he felt uncomfortable with his rather passive position, which in turn led to an oversight on move 27.

White: Karpov
Black: Korchnoi

Caro-Kann Defence

1	P-K4	P-QB3

The Caro-Kann was called the poor man's opening in the good old days, in spite of the successes of players like Capablanca and Nimzowitsch. Later Flohr played it with virtuosity, and when Botvinnik was too old to play his complicated variation in the French Defence against the sorcerer from Riga, Mikhail Tal, he turned to the solid Caro-Kann and won his title back. Smyslov and Petrosian have played it consistently, and in 1974 Karpov surprised Spassky with it in their Candidates' semi-final.

But is it an opening for Korchnoi? Well, it can be just as good as the French in game sixteen .....

From a fighter who is three games behind you might expect 5...NPxN, but Korchnoi has probably decided that he must try to draw with Black and play for a win with the white pieces. Bronstein has played 5...KPxN quite often. Once I was looking at his game and he thought he could see criticism in my face. He stood up and explained to me that he know he ought to play something else, but he was not feeling well and hoped to get a quick draw with this variation.

Keene has been writing about the Caro-Kann lately. He thinks 5...KPxN is okay and quotes some games by Ulf Andersson.

2	P-Q4	P-Q4
3	N-Q2	PxP
4	NxP	N-KB3
5	NxNch	KPxN

6	B-QB4	N-Q2

Andersson plays 6...Q-K2ch 7 Q-K2 B-K3, or 7...B-N5. Also 6...B-Q3 is more common than the text move.

7	N-K2	B-Q3
8	0-0	0-0
9	B-B4	N-N3
10	B-Q3	B-K3
11	P-QB3	N-Q4
12	BxB	QxB
13	Q-Q2	QR-Q1
14	KR-K1	P-KN3
15	QR-Q1	K-N2

Black's position looks solid, but an active plan is difficult to find. Karpov patiently prepares the advance of his pawn majority on the Q-side.

16	B-K4	N-B2
17	P-QN3	KR-K1
18	B-N1	B-N5
19	P-KR3	BxN
20	RxB	RxR
21	QxR	N-Q4
22	Q-Q2	N-B5
23	B-K4	P-KB4
24	B-B3	P-KR3

24...P-KN4 was possible.

25	P-KR4	N-K3
26	Q-K3	N-B2
27	P-B4	P-B5?

Either Korchnoi was getting desperate or he overlooked White's 29th move. 27...P-N3 was natural, with only a slight plus for White.

28	Q-B3	Q-B3

29	Q-R5!	N-K3
30	P-Q5	PxP
31	PxP	P-N3
32	Q-R4	

Stronger than 32 QxRP N-Q5.

32	...	N-B4
33	QxRP	N-Q2
34	P-Q6	QxRP
35	Q-B7	

To delay the advance of the black pawns on the K-side. 35 P-QN4 P-KN4 is unclear.

35	...	Q-B3
36	P-QN4	P-R4
37	P-R4	K-R3
38	P-N5	P-N4
39	B-B6	N-B4
40	P-Q7	K-N2
41	R-K1	N-K3

Adjourned, but it would probably have been a good idea for Karpov to seal his previous move.

42 Q-Q6

After half an hour's thought.

42 QxP! looks like a win. For instance: 42...P-N5 43 P-R5 P-N6 44 PxP PxP (threatening ...N-Q5) 45 Q-K3 Q-R5 46 P-R6. After 46...N-B5 47 P-R7, the rook pawn is just in time to prevent Black from taking the QP. Another attempt for Black is 43...Q-B6 (instead of 43...P-N6), hoping for the perpetual check 44 RxN?PxR 45 QxR Q-K8ch 46 K-R2 P-N6ch 47 PxP QxNPch, etc., but after 43...Q-B6 44 R-KB1! P-R5 45 P-R6 P-R6 46 P-R7 PxP 47 BxP P-B6 48 QxR PxB 49 Q-KN8ch! KxQ 50 P-R8=Qch K-N2 51 QxP, the white RP has once again arrived at exactly the right moment, just like the U.S. Cavalry saving the fort in all those old Hollywood movies. Still another idea, after 42 QxP! P-N5 43 P-R5, is 43...P-B6 44 PxP N-Q5 45 R-K8 RxP! 46 BxR NxBPch, with some drawing chances, but White can play much more simply with 44 Q-K3, threatening the exchange of queens.

So in several variations White's

win hangs on one tempo, but it seems to be there all the time.

42	...	P-N5
43	K-B1	P-N6
44	Q-K5	

White has lost a tempo as compared with 42 Q-K5, or so it seems. But after 42 Q-K5 Black would have played 42...QxQ 43 RxQ K-B3, followed by ...K-K2, with good drawing chances.

44	...	P-R5
45	P-R5	QNPxP
46	P-N6	QxQ
47	RxQ	R-QN1
48	P-N7	N-Q1
49	R-K8	

There is no win in 49 B-B3 K-B3 50 RxP K-K2 51 R-R8 RxP 52 BxR NxB 53 P-B3 (to keep two pawns on the board) 53...N-Q1! (to defend the pawn on KB5) 54 R-R5 KxP 55 R-R5 N-K3 56 RxP K-Q3 57 R-R5 N-Q5, followed by ...P-B4.

49	...	K-B3
50	PxP	BPxP
51	K-K2	K-N2

52 B-B3??

Stop. Annotator wake up! It is too easy to take it for granted that Karpov's team has seen everything and that there was no win after his sealed move. But really, Black's rook and knight are immobilized, so why should White not win? His king can take the QRP, his bishop can stop the K-side pawns. Why not a move like 52 K-Q2 may I ask? Black's counterplay must lie in a combination of the advance of all his pawns and when the white king goes to the QN-file Black can play ...RxP with check.

Let us try: 52 K-Q2 P-B4 53 K-B3 P-B5 54 K-N2 P-R6 55 PxP RxPch (if 55...NxB 56 RxR P-N7 57 R-N8ch KxR 58 P-N8 = Qch NxQ 59 P-Q8 = Qch) 56 BxR NxB 57 R-QN8! and wins. With the black pawn on ...KB2 instead of ...KB4 White would play 57 R-K3, or if Black tries 53...K-B3 (instead of 53...P-B5) White would win with (54 K-N2 P-R6 55 PxP RxPch 56 BxR NxB) 57 R-KN8 P-B5 58 P-R4 K-K2 59 P-R5 KxP 60 P-R6 N-Q3 61 P-R7 N-B2 62 R-N7.

If Black does nothing the white king goes to QR3, then comes B-B3 and K-R4-N5-N6, winning. So 52 K-Q2 wins!

But there is more. Even 52 K-B3 P-B4 53 K-B4 K-B3 54 B-Q5 wins! After 54...P-R5 55 R-K5 P-QR6 56 R-K2 Black is in zugzwang. Tal gives 56...K-N3 57 R-R2 (even 57 K-K5 wins) 57...K-B3 58 RxP K-K2 59 R-R8 RxP 60 BxR NxB 61 R-R8 KxP 62 KxP and the two black pawns are doomed.

Karpov thought for 20 minutes. He had to choose between two plans,

both of which win. In the end he made a "natural" move which does not .....

52 ...   P-R5!
53 R-K4

It is too late for 53 K-Q3 P-QR6 54 K-B2 P-B4! The point is that the white king has to choose between two bad squares. QN1 is bad because Black queens with check. QN3 is bad because of the knight check on ...QB4: 55 K-N3 P-R6 56 PxP RxPch 57 BxR NxB, and 58 R-QN8 does not work because of that check.

53 ...   K-B3
54 RxQRP   K-K2

What a difference. The king helps the other two pieces to fight against the passed pawns. 55 R-R8 RxP 56 BxR NxB 57 R-R8 KxP 58 RxP, followed by the win of the NP, is not enough for White to win.

55	RxP	KxP
56	R-KB4	K-Q3
57	R-QN4	K-B2
58	R-QB4ch	K-Q2
59	B-N4ch	K-K1
60	R-K4ch	K-B1
61	B-Q7	RxP!

Not 61...NxP 62 R-QN4, and White wins because of the pin.

62	R-K8ch	K-N2
63	RxN	R-N7ch
	Drawn	

Because of 64 K-B3 R-Q7, when White cannot get out of the pin.

Korchnoi's advisers on meditation taught him a very simple trick to improve concentration during play: splash your eyes with cold water! It is not clear if it helped him, but he did catch a cold...

GAME TWENTY-ONE
12th and 13th September

The match comes alive again! If Karpov had won the previous game it would have been 5-1 and almost over. Now it is 4-2 and a tired looking World Champion keeps the match exciting. Korchnoi was in great spirits after the game and quoted from the bible: "Father, forgive them, for they know not what they do". It is not clear what he meant by this, probably nothing special, but certainly not that Black could have held the adjourned game.

Maybe Korchnoi is learning something from the gurus. He had twenty minutes for his last eight moves before the first time control, even though Karpov's surprising tenth move would have been sufficient reason for the challenger to spend almost all of his time on his reply and the next few moves.

White: Korchnoi
Black: Karpov

Queen's Gambit Declined

1	P-QB4	N-KB3
2	N-QB3	P-K3
3	N-B3	P-Q4
4	P-Q4	B-K2
5	B-B4	0-0
6	P-K3	P-B4
7	QPxP	BxP
8	Q-B2	N-B3
9	R-Q1	Q-R4
10	P-QR3	R-K1!?

So far as I know, this move is a novelty. Apart from 10...B-K2 (as in game nine) the known continuations are 10...N-K5 and 10...R-Q1. The first of these got a fat question mark about 15 years ago, after (for instance) the game Portisch-Berger, Amsterdam Interzonal 1964: 10...N-K5 11 PxP NxN 12 NPxN PxP 13 N-N5 P-KN3 14 RxP QxRP 15 B-B4 N-Q1 16 NxRP! KxN 17 R-R5ch K-N2 18 B-K5ch P-B3 19 R-N5! and Black resigned.

After 10...R-Q1 11 N-Q2 P-Q5?! 12 N-N3 Q-N3 13 N-R4 B-N5ch 14 PxB QxPch 15 N-Q2 Q-R4 16 P-QN3, White refutes the black attack, and after 11...PxP (instead of

11...P-Q5?!) White gets a slight initiative.

Karpov's move is perfectly logical, with the white king still in the centre. White cannot play 11 P-QN4? because of 11...NxP! 12 PxN BxNP.

11	N-Q2	P-K4
12	B-N5	N-Q5!?

Karpov is not light-hearted when it comes to sacrifices, so the annotator can take it for granted that 13 PxN PxPch 14 N-K2 is bad for White. But what if the reader wants proof? The white position looks miserable, but how does Black continue the attack? 14...N-K5 15 B-R4 PxP 16 QxP B-K3 is nice, but not absolutely convincing. 14...N-N5! is stronger: 15 B-R4 (the threat was 15...NxBP 16 KxN

P-Q6ch, winning the queen) 15...PxP, for instance 16 P-QN4 PxPe.p. 17 QxNP B-K3, or 16 QxBP B-K3 or 16...N-K4, winning for Black in each case. In most variations either the black knight or the pawn gets to ...Q6 with disastrous consequences.

13	Q-N1!	B-B4
14	B-Q3	P-K5
15	B-B2	NxBch
16	QxN	Q-R3

A little disappointing after the previous series of aggressive moves, but 16...P-Q5 17 BxN PxB 18 N-Q5 P-Q6 19 Q-N3 is in White's favour, in spite of the advanced black QP.

17	BxN	QxB
18	N-N3!	B-Q3

19 RxP!

19 NxQP? Q-N3 would have given Black good compensation for the pawn. Now he gets no attack after 19...Q-N3 20 0-0 (but not 20 P-B4? PxPe.p.! 21 RxB(B5) RxPch 22 K-Q1 PxP 23 R-N1 QR-K1) 20...Q-R3 21 P-R3 BxKRP 22 RxB! QxR 23 PxB.

19	...	R-K4
20	N-Q4	R-QB1

21	RxR	QxR

Not 21...BxR? 22 N-Q5 Q-K3 23 NxB.

22	NxB	QxN(B4)
23	0-0	

Safest. 23 QxP? QxQ 24 NxQ RxP 25 N-B3 BxQRP! is out of the question, while 23 NxP P-QN4 also gives Black chances.

23	...	RxP
24	R-Q1!	

Stronger than 24 Q-N3 Q-B1. But now Karpov misses the best defence: after 24...B-K2!, White has only a very slight edge, for instance 25 P-B3 P-KR3 26 PxP. Instead of 25 P-B3, 25 R-Q4 RxR 26 PxR B-B3!, is satisfactory for Black.

24	...	Q-K4
25	P-KN3	P-QR3

26 Q-N3 was a strong threat.

26 Q-N3

26 R-Q4 RxR 27 PxR QxQP 28 NxP B-B1 is tenable for Black.

26	...	P-QN4

27	P-QR4	R-N5

There is nothing better. The black position reminds me of some white positions in the Meran Variation of the Slav Defence, when the attack peters out and the advanced centre pawn is just a weakness.

28	Q-Q5	QxQ
29	RxQ	B-B1
30	PxP	P-QR4

30...PxP 31 RxP, and 30...RxP(N7) 31 PxP are hopeless. Now White could get an ending with four pawns against three on the K-side: 31 P-N6 RxP(N3) 32 RxP RxP 33 NxP. In a pure rook ending this is a draw, and with rook and bishop against rook and knight also. But exactly the combination of rook and knight against rook and bishop offers good winning chances.

Korchnoi, however, chooses to hold on to his passed pawn, and he was probably right. As I have already mentioned, he had plenty of time for this decision.

31	R-Q8	RxP(N7)
32	R-R8	P-B4

Or 32...R-N6 33 N-Q5, threatening N-K7ch.

33	RxP	B-N5
34	R-R8ch	K-B2
35	N-R4	

This looks like a bad square for the knight, but the important thing was to drive the black rook away from the attack on ...KB7.

35	...	R-N8ch
36	K-N2	B-Q3
37	R-R7ch	K-B3
38	P-N6	B-N1

The position is quite tricky. Against 38... R-N6, 39 R-QB7 looks good, but in fact it is bad because of 39...R-N5!. Correct is 39 R-Q7 B-K4 40 P-B4, reaching positions similar to the game continuation.

39	R-R8	B-K4
40	N-B5	B-Q3
41	P-N7	

White is making progress, but since I did not find a clear improvement for Black on move 38 I did not put a question mark after ...B-N1.

41	...	K-K2
42	R-KN8	B-K4

42...K-B2? 43 R-Q8 loses at once (43...B-K4 44 R-Q5).

Here the game was adjourned. Korchnoi sealed his next move.

43 P-B4!

The white king comes out of his prison.

43 ...   PxPe.p.ch
44 KxP   K-B2

Or 44...R-N4 45 N-Q3 K-B2 46 R-Q8 K-K2 47 NxB!, and wins.

45 R-QB8   K-K2
46 P-R3!

This move creates fresh possibilities. After an eventual P-N4 PxPch; PxP, White gets the use of the K4 square for his king, his knight or his KP, or probably all three. Black cannot prevent this with 46...P-N3 47 P-N4 R-N4, because of 48 PxP PxP 49 N-Q3 B-Q3 50 R-KR8. But 46...P-N3 47 P-N4 PxPch 48 PxP P-R4 was probably Black's best chance. In fact it looks so good that White may have to play 48 KxP instead of PxP.

46 ...   P-R4?
47 R-KN8!   K-B2

Forced, because of the threat 48 N-Q3 K-B2 49 R-Q8 K-K2 50 NxB!

48 R-Q8   P-N4

To answer N-Q3 with ...P-N5ch.
Why not 48...K-K2 again? And why did White not go to Q8 with the rook on move 45? The answer lies in the variation 48...K-K2 49 R-Q7ch K-K1 (49...K-B3 50 R-Q5 B-B2 51 N-R6! RxP 52 R-Q7) 50 R-Q5 B-N1 51 RxP, attacking the RP and winning easily. With the pawn on ...KR2

Black would play ...B-Q3 in this position, and against N-K4 he would play ...B-K2. White would still have winning chances, but it would be difficult to make progress because the exchange of minor pieces leads to a rook ending which is a draw by good defence, as for instance in a radio game J. Nielsen-Z. Nilsson, 1949! I am probably getting old, since I remember these games from my childhood better than most games from recent tournaments.

Now White can win a piece with 49 N-Q7, but after 49...P-N5ch 50 PxP BPxPch 51 K-K4 BxP, Black would get drawing chances.

49 P-N4!   RPxPch

49...BPxPch 50 PxP P-R5 51 N-Q7 K-K2 52 P-N8=Q RxQ 53 RxR KxN 54 R-N8 B-B3 55 K-K4 K-K3 56 R-N6 K-B2 57 K-B5, is hopeless for Black.

50 PxP   K-K2
51 R-KN8   PxPch
52 KxP   K-B2
53 R-QB8

After 53 RxP? B-Q3 54 N-K4 B-K2, Black draws. With so few pawns left White must be careful.

53	...	B-Q3
54	P-K4	

Not 54 KxP? BxN!

Now 54...BxN does not hold, and White is threatening KxP followed by the king march to the Q-side. 54...B-B5 55 K-B5, threatening P-K5, is no improvement.

54	...	R-N8ch
55	K-B5	P-N5

Desperate. White can win with 56 P-N8=Q BxQ 57 RxB P-N6 58 R-N7ch, and with 56 R-Q8 B-R7 57 R-Q7ch K-K1 58 R-N7 (or 58 P-K5). Korchnoi finds another solution, nicely calculated.

56	P-K5	R-KB8ch
57	K-K4	R-K8ch
58	K-Q5	R-Q8ch

Or 58...BxP 59 N-Q3 R-QN8 60 NxB (with check!)

59	N-Q3	RxNch
60	K-B4	Resigns

One of the better games of the match.

Petrosian
1963-1969

Spassky
1969-1972

GAME TWENTY-TWO
14th September

Like game 20 this one might have decided the match, or at least given Karpov his fifth victory. If the champion had adjourned at move 41 he would undoubtedly have won easily. Instead he made seven more moves and threw away the win.

White: Karpov
Black: Korchnoi

French Defence

1	P-K4 ·	P-K3
2	P-Q4	P-Q4
3	N-Q2	P-QB4
4	KPxP	KPxP
5	B-N5ch	B-Q2
6	Q-K2ch	B-K2

More interesting than 6...Q-K2 (game 16).

7	PxP	N-KB3
8	N-N3	0-0
9	B-K3	R-K1
10	N-B3	BxP
11	NxB	

11 B(N5)xB QNxB 12 NxB NxN 13 Q-N5! R-QB1 14 0-0, gives White a microscopic advantage.

11	...	Q-R4ch
12	Q-Q2	QxB
13	0-0-0	

13	...	P-QN3

This looks like loss of time. The natural continuation is 13...B-N5. Korchnoi must have been afraid of 14 B-Q4 N-K5 15 Q-B4 BxN 16 PxB NxN 17 BxP KxB 18 KR-N1ch K-B1 19 Q-Q6ch! R-K2 20 Q-KR6ch K-K1 21 R-N8ch K-Q2 22 RxPch K-B2 23 Q-Q6 mate!! This is not forced, but after 15...NxN 16 QxB Black's position is no better than in the game.

14	NxB	QNxN
15	K-N1	N-K5

Probably not satisfied with the position, Korchnoi provokes the exchange of queens he avoided on move 6. I would prefer 15...N-B4.

16	Q-Q3	QxQ
17	RxQ	N(Q2)-B3
18	P-KR3	N-B4
19	R(Q3)-Q1	N-K3
20	P-B3	P-QN4
21	N-Q4	P-QR3
22	N-B2	P-QR4
23	R-Q3	QR-N1
24	KR-Q1	P-R3(?)

Probably better would be 24...R(N1)-B1 or 24...P-R4.

25	P-KB4!?	R(N1)-B1

25...P-N3 26 P-B5 was obviously very unpleasant. Now 26 P-B5 already gives White good winning chances, for instance 26...N-B4 27

108

BxN RxB 28 N-K3 R-K4 29 P-QN4. But Karpov's continuation is even stronger.

| 26 | P-KN4! | P-Q5! |

The best chance. 27 NxP N-B4 gives Black the exchange for two pawns.

| 27 | PxP | N-Q4 |
| 28 | R-KB1 | P-N5 |

28...RxN 29 KxR N-N5ch 30 K-Q2 NxR 31 KxN N-B2 32 B-Q2 N-Q4 33 R-B1, offers Black no drawing chances.

| 29 | B-Q2 |

| 29 | ... | R-K2? |

Much better 29...N(K3)-B2, with some compensation for the pawn.

| 30 | P-B5 | N-N4 |
| 31 | N-K3! | |

White gives back the pawn, to break the blockade of the QP.

31	...	N-B3
32	P-Q5	NxRP
33	P-Q6	R-Q2
34	N-Q5!	NxN

35	RxN(Q5)	R-R1
36	B-K3	N-N4
37	B-N6	N-K5
38	R(B1)-Q1	

Not 38 BxP?? RxB!

38	...	P-R5
39	R(Q5)-Q4	R-K1
40	RxP	RxP
41	RxR	NxR

The only one who can prevent White from winning this position is - Karpov!

Simplest was 42 RxP with two united passed pawns. Black's 42...P-R4 was not to be taken seriously. ("Karpov could seal 42 RxP and Black resigns" - Stean)

42	B-B7?!	R-K8ch
43	K-B2	N-K1
44	B-R5	P-R6
45	R-N8	R-K2
46	B-N4??	

46 PxP won. 46 P-N4 won.

| 46 | ... | R-K7ch |
| 47 | K-Q3 | PxP |

The sealed move. It still looks like a win for White, but there are some difficulties. 48 B-B3 P-N8=Qch! 49

RxQ RxP 50 R-N8 R-KN7 51 RxNch K-R2 is a draw! For instance 52 R-K4 P-R4 53 PxP R-KR7 54 R-KN4 P-B3 55 K-K4 RxP. When the white rook leaves the KN-file, ...P-N3 exchanges the last white pawn.

48	B-Q2	R-K2
49	P-R4	R-Q2ch
50	K-B2	K-R2
51	RxP	P-R4!
52	PxP	N-Q3

Threatening ...N-B5, one of the ideas behind 49...R-Q2ch.

53	R-R2	NxP
54	P-R5	N-Q5ch
55	K-B3	

Or 55 K-N1 N-N6 56 B-K3 NxP 57 RxN P-N3 58 P-R6 P-B3 59 R-R2 P-N4 60 R-R2 K-N3 61 B-B5 R-Q1, followed by ...R-KR1.

55	...	N-B3
56	P-R6	R-Q4
57	B-B4	R-KB4

Not 57...RxP 58 R-R2!

58	B-Q6	R-Q4
59	B-N3	R-KN4

Against 60 B-B7 Black has ...R-QB4ch ready.

60	B-B2	RxP
61	K-B4	N-R4ch
62	K-B3	N-B3
63	K-B4	N-R4ch
64	K-B3	N-B3
	Drawn	

Fischer
1972-1975

GAME TWENTY-THREE
16th September

When this game was over, Korchnoi remained sitting on the stage. "Where did I go wrong?" he asked Lothar Schmid. He then pointed out a win on move 38, but there is no win. Earlier White could have chosen various other variations, which seem to offer some winning chances. But a clear win is impossible to demonstrate, and the game as a whole is really a remarkable defence by Karpov.

White: Korchnoi
Black: Karpov

Queen's Gambit Declined

1	P-QB4	N-KB3
2	N-QB3	P-K3
3	N-B3	P-Q4
4	P-Q4	B-K2
5	B-B4	0-0
6	P-K3	P-B4
7	QPxP	BxP
8	Q-B2	N-B3
9	R-Q1	Q-R4
10	P-QR3	B-K2

The interesting experiment 10...R-K1 is not repeated.

11	N-Q2	P-K4
12	B-N5	P-Q5
13	N-N3	Q-N3

Seen before, but 13...Q-Q1, as in game nine, is more common.

14	BxN	BxB
15	N-Q5	Q-Q1
16	B-Q3	P-KN3
17	PxP	NxP
18	NxN	PxN
19	NxBch	QxN
20	0-0	B-K3

This looks better than 20...B-Q2, which was played in Forintos-Smederevac, Wijk aan Zee 1970. But still the general impression is that the black QP is solidly blockaded while White's pawn majority may go places.

21	KR-K1	QR-B1
22	P-QN3	KR-Q1
23	B-K4	R-B2
24	Q-Q2	B-N5

24...P-N3 is probably better.

25	P-B3	B-K3
26	P-QR4!	P-N3

111

27 P-R5 P-QN4!?

Very courageous defence. The move required good judgement since it was not absolutely necessary. After other moves Black would have an isolated QNP and some slight difficulties, but probably a tenable position. Instead of defending carefully for a long time, Karpov forces a crisis.

28 PxP BxP
29 R-N1 B-Q4

Not 29...R-B6? 30 P-N6! (and if 30...PxP 31 P-R6!).

30 P-N6

30 BxB RxB 31 R-K8ch K-N2 32 P-N6 PxP 33 RxP Q-N4! leads nowhere.

30 ... PxP
31 RxP R-B3
32 RxR

Not 32 BxB RxB 33 R-K8ch K-N2 34 R(N6)-N8 P-R4, and if 35 R-KR8 Q-N4!.

32 ... BxR
33 B-Q3 B-Q2!

Fine defence. To make the black

QP as strong as the white QRP Black has to exchange the blockading bishop.

34 P-R6

Or 34 R-R1 B-B4 35 BxB P-Q6.

34 ... B-B4
35 Q-B4 K-N2
36 BxB QxB
37 QxQ PxQ

38 R-R1

Korchnoi said that he should have played 38 K-B2, but 38...P-Q6 still draws. Also against 38 P-R7. If the white rook were on Q1, 38 P-R7 would win.

38 ... P-Q6
39 K-B2 R-K1!

Cutting off the white king, and thereby ensuring the exchange of the two passed pawns.

40 R-R2 R-K2!
41 R-Q2

Or 41 P-R7 P-Q7.

41 ... R-K3
Drawn

The open Ruy again! I believe Korchnoi should have kept playing it in spite of his defeat in game 14; it agrees with his style. But of course he did not want to repeat game 14, so he played 9...B-K2 instead of B-QB4. Karpov's 11th was rather passive, and Black came out of the opening with an even game. In the ending he tried to win, but it was not too difficult for White to draw.

So, 24 games played, the maximum number under the rules 1951-1972. How many more? Some Philippine journalists are writing that the government ought to pay each player $100,000 for leaving .....

White: Karpov
Black: Korchnoi

Ruy Lopez

1	P-K4	P-K4
2	N-KB3	N-QB3
3	B-N5	P-QR3
4	B-R4	N-B3
5	0-0	NxP
6	P-Q4	P-QN4
7	B-N3	P-Q4
8	PxP	B-K3
9	P-B3	B-K2
10	B-B2	N-B4

10...0-0 is normal. The position after the text move could be reached with 9...N-B4 10 B-B2 B-K2, but Korchnoi was probably afraid of 10 N-Q4.

11 P-KR3

Stopping ...B-N5, but it looks like a wasted tempo in other continuations. However, after 11 R-K1 B-N5 Karpov would not get an early N-Q4, which is obviously his favourite manoeuvre in this type of position.

11	...	0-0
12	R-K1	Q-Q2
13	N-Q4	NxN
14	PxN	N-N2
15	N-Q2	P-QB4

Strangely enough Korchnoi spent 25 minutes on this move. It is difficult to find another plan in the position.

16	PxP	NxP
17	N-B3	B-B4!

Not a real pawn sacrifice, for after 18 BxB QxB 19 QxP KR-Q1 20 Q-B6 N-Q6 Black wins back the pawn at once, for example 21 Q-K4 QxQ 22 RxQ QR-B1. 20...QR-B1 is less clear after 21 Q-QN6 N-Q6 22 R-B1 B-B4 23 QxRP BxPch or 23...NxBP 24 P-QN4!

After the exchange of bishops White has no attacking chances on the K-side. The isolated black QP is a weakness, but so is the (too) far advanced white KP and Black has active pieces.

18	B-K3	QR-B1

18...BxB 19 QxB QR-B1 was more natural.

19	QR-B1	BxB
20	RxB	N-K3
21	R-Q2	KR-Q1

21...B-N5 22 RxP Q-B3 23 R-K2! KR-Q1 24 RxRch RxR 25 Q-B2 gives Black nothing for the pawn.

22	Q-N3	R-B5
23	R(K1)-Q1	Q-N2
24	P-R3	P-N3
25	Q-R2	P-QR4

Korchnoi had 35 minutes left, Karpov 70.

26	P-QN3	R-B6
27	P-QR4	PxP

27...B-N5 looks interesting; against 28 Q-N2, 28...P-Q5 is strong (29 NxP Q-K5!). But White plays 28 R-Q3!, and against 28...RxR 29 RxR P-Q5 he has 30 NxP! B-B4? 31 NxN!

28	PxP	R-B5
29	P-Q3	K-N2

29...Q-B3 looks more natural, but White has the defence 30 N-Q4.

30	Q-Q2	RxP
31	B-R6ch	K-N1
32	RxP	RxR
33	QxR	QxQ
34	RxQ	B-B1
35	BxB	KxB
36	P-N3	K-K2

37	R-N5	N-B2
38	R-B5	N-K3
39	R-N5	N-Q1

Playing for a win? At least it seems he couldn't make up his mind to be satisfied with a draw before the time control.

40	K-N2	P-R3
41	N-Q2	R-R8

Adjourned. Some commentators saw some slight winning chances for Black, due to his passed pawn. But White's knight and rook are well placed, and he should not have any trouble drawing. The game could have been agreed drawn, except Korchnoi might have been hoping for 42 N-N3? R-QN8 .....

42	N-B4	N-B3
43	R-B5	K-Q2
44	N-N6ch	K-B2
45	N-B8(!)	Drawn

After 45...KxN the rook ending is a dead draw.

GAME TWENTY-FIVE
23rd and 24th September

This game should have been played two days earlier, but Karpov had it postponed because an aeroplane dived over his hotel at 9.00 a.m. and woke him up. When the game got going two days later, Karpov's play on moves 36-38 were reminiscent of that dive. Up to move 35 this was really one of Karpov's best performances in the match. But when the game was adjourned after move 41, it was sheer luck that he could still draw it.

White: Korchnoi
Black: Karpov

English Opening

1	P-QB4	N-KB3
2	N-QB3	P-K4

No Queen's Gambit this time.

3	P-KN3	B-N5
4	Q-N3	

Korchnoi has often played this with Black (1 P-K4 P-QB4 2 N-KB3 N-QB3 3 B-N5 Q-N3), but it is not clear that it is one of White's best moves. There are even some continuations where the move P-KN3 is of doubtful value.

4	...	N-B3
5	N-Q5	

After 5 P-K3 BxN 6 QxB P-Q4 Black takes the initiative.

5	...	B-B4
6	P-K3	0-0
7	B-N2	NxN
8	PxN	N-K2
9	N-K2	P-Q3
10	0-0	P-QB3

The equalizer.

11	P-Q4	KPxP
12	KPxP	B-N3

13	B-N5	B-Q2
14	P-QR4	P-KR3
15	BxN	QxB
16	B-B3 (?)	

16 KR-K1 KR-K1 (17 P-R5? BxQP!) is just as uncomfortable for White, but 16 P-R5 QxN 17 PxB RPxP 18 QxP Q-N4, with a drawish ending, was correct. Korchnoi spent lots of time around here, but found nothing and ought to have satisfied himself with a peaceful conclusion.

16	...	QR-N1
17	P-R5	B-B2
18	Q-B3	KR-B1
19	N-B4	B-Q1
20	KR-K1	Q-B1

At the moment Black's position looks passive, but this is a case where Tarrasch can be quoted, for the future belongs to the bishop pair.

21	Q-N3	B-N4
22	N-K2	B-B3
23	QR-Q1	P-B4
24	B-K4	

A rather strange move, but Black is better already. Korchnoi had less than a minute per move now.

24	...	Q-Q1
25	Q-R2	B-N5
26	PxP	RxP
27	P-N4	R-B2
28	Q-N3	R(N1)-B1
29	P-B3	B-Q2
30	Q-K3	P-R3
31	B-Q3	B-N7
32	K-N2	Q-B3
33	R-QN1	B-R5

With the two bishops and control of the most important open file Black has a won game.

34	N-B4	P-KN3
35	R-K2(?)	B-B8
36	Q-K4	

Karpov played quickly, which is not advisable when you have the advantage. Did he forget 36...R-K1, or did he think there was an even easier win in the position?

36	...	K-B1?!

37	P-N5	PxP
38	Q-N4	R-B4?

38...BxN ought to win rather easily, for instance 39 QxB(B4) QxQ 40 PxQ R-B4 41 R(K2)-N2 B-B7! (not 41...RxP 42 B-K4).

In spite of his acute time pressure, Korchnoi saw his chance. Maybe he did not calculate everything, but it was now or never.

39	RxB!	RxR
40	NxPch!	K-N2

40...PxN 41 R-K6 wins for White, e.g. 41...R(B1)-B7ch 42 K-R3! Q-Q1 43 RxQP Q-B1ch 44 R-Q7ch K-N1 (44...R-B4 45 Q-KB4ch) 45 Q-K7 and Black must play 45...QxRch, which is hopeless.

For once the last move before the time control was the best!

41	N-K7	R(B1)-B5

41...R-Q1 still offered winning chances, or so I read. But after 42 Q-N4ch K-R1 43 Q-K4 or 42...Q-N4 43 Q-Q4ch, White has at least a draw.

Korchnoi sealed his next move.

42	BxR	RxB
43	QxQP!	R-B6!

After 43...QxQ 44 N-B5ch K-B1 45 NxQ, White would have a winning advantage. The game continuation is one or two tempi better for Black.

43...B-Q8 looks strong but would have been a mistake. After 44 QxQch KxQ 45 N-N8ch K-N2 46 R-Q2 BxPch 47 KxB KxN 48 P-Q6 R-B1 49 K-K4, White would win the rook ending, and 46...B-R5 47 P-Q6 P-N5 48 NxP! B-Q2 49 N-B5ch! is no better.

44	P-B4	QxQ
45	N-B5ch	K-N3
46	NxQ	B-N6

Thanks to his 43rd move Black is threatening to take the white QP with check, instead of having to move his rook out of reach of the white knight.

47	P-B5ch	K-N2
48	N-K8ch	K-B1
49	N-B6	K-N2
50	N-R5ch	K-B1
51	N-B4	B-B5
52	R-K5	

52 R-Q2 P-N5 53 P-Q6 K-K1 54 N-Q5 BxNch 55 RxB offers White some winning chances - but after 52...K-K1! (53 P-Q6 K-Q2 54 N-Q5? R-Q6!) Black has no problems.

52	...	R-R6
53	P-Q6	R-R7ch
54	K-B3	R-Q7
55	R-K7	RxQP
56	RxNP	R-R3
57	R-N6	RxP
58	RxRP	P-N5
59	R-QB6	B-N4

| 60 | R-B1 | P-N6 |
| 61 | R-QN1 | B-B5 |

The black passed pawn is too strong - White cannot win.

62	K-K4	R-R7
63	K-Q4	R-QB7
64	N-Q3	BxN
65	KxB	RxP
66	RxP	K-N2

The game is a dead draw, but it is a good old rule that the player who is a pawn down should at least suffer a little.

67	K-K4	R-R7
68	K-B4	R-R5ch
69	K-N5	R-R4
70	P-N4	R-B4
71	K-R5	R-R4
72	R-KB3	R-N4
73	P-N5	R-N8
74	P-B6ch	K-R2
75	R-KR3	R-N8
76	R-R2	R-N6
77	R-R1	R-N7
78	R-R1	R-KR7ch
79	K-N4	K-N3
80	R-R8	R-KN7ch
	Drawn	

GAME TWENTY-SIX
26th September

For the second time in the match Karpov plays the English Opening. The result is a rather quiet and a rather correct game, almost like game six. Was that the World Champion's intention? A Russian source said that Karpov had been sleeping badly for quite some time. He now moved away from his hotel to a villa in the mountains; he complained about noise. The decision to move out was reportedly caused by a lawn-mower.

White: Karpov
Black: Korchnoi

English Opening

1	P-QB4	P-K4
2	N-QB3	P-Q3
3	P-KN3	P-KB4
4	B-N2	N-QB3
5	P-Q3	N-B3
6	P-K3	B-K2

So it is "Classical Dutch against English", not a normal "Closed Sicilian Reversed".

7	KN-K2	0-0
8	0-0	Q-K1
9	P-B4	B-Q1
10	P-QR3	R-N1
11	P-QN4	B-K3
12	N-Q5	

12 B-Q2, intending R-B1 followed by N-Q5, was slower. Black could prevent this with ...Q-B2 or ...N-K2.

12	...	P-QN4

Surprising and good.

13	B-N2	NPxP
14	QPxP	P-K5
15	NxNch	BxN
16	BxB	RxB
17	R-B1	P-QR4!

Not 17...Q-B2 18 P-B5 with a clear advantage for White.

18	P-N5	N-Q1
19	R-KB2	N-N2
20	B-B1	N-B4
21	N-B3	B-B2
22	N-Q5	

Other possibilities were 22 R-Q2 (probably best) and 22 N-R4 B-R4 23 Q-B2 P-B3 24 R-Q2 N-Q6! or 24 NxN! PxN 25 R-Q2, with advantage

118

for White. But 23...R-K3!, threatening ...N-Q6, is better. After 24 NxN PxN Black gains control of the Q-file, which gives him good chances even if he loses the QRP.

| 22 | ... | BxN |
| 23 | PxB | |

Black has a good knight against a not very active bishop. His only problem is the weak QRP, for

instance 23...P-R3 24 R-QN2 K-R2 25 Q-Q2 R-R1 26 P-N6 with advantage for White.

Korchnoi decides to play for a draw.

23	...	N-Q6!?
24	BxN	PxB
25	QxP	QxNP
26	QxQ	RxQ
27	RxP	R-B2!

Not 27...RxP? 28 R-QN2! with some winning chances for White.

Drawn

Because of 28 R-B8ch R-B1 29 RxRch KxR 30 R-Q2(?) R-N6.

Especially White's 22nd and Black's 23rd indicate that neither player was in the mood for risks and experiments after the ups and downs of the 25th game.

Karpov
1975-??

28th September

A very strange game. Korchnoi gets a slight advantage in a well-known variation of the Sicilian Reversed. Then he starts playing without a plan! As a result, Karpov equalizes and a draw would be the logical result. But, short of time, Korchnoi continues making second and third best moves. From an advantageous position at move 19, he manages to get into a difficult position by move 29, and a lost one by move 31. A very weak performance by the challenger, reminiscent of the first part of game 25: no idea, no plans; just fatigue.

White: Korchnoi
Black: Karpov

English Opening

1	P-QB4	N-KB3
2	N-QB3	P-K4
3	N-B3	N-B3
4	P-KN3	B-N5
5	N-Q5	NxN

Objectively, 5...B-B4 is probably better. My guess is that Karpov was playing for a draw and thought that it was a good idea to get the knights out of the way.

6	PxN	N-Q5
7	NxN	

7 NxP? Q-K2 8 P-B4 P-Q3 9 N-Q3 Q-K5 is unplayable for White.

7	...	PxN
8	Q-B2	

Threatening to win a pawn, for instance 8...0-0? 9 Q-B4.

8	...	Q-K2

9 QxP Q-K5 is good for Black.

9	B-N2	B-B4
10	0-0	0-0
11	P-K3	B-N3(?)

11...P-Q3 was the natural move.

12	P-QR4	PxP
13	QPxP	P-QR4
14	B-Q2	B-B4
15	B-QB3	P-Q3
16	Q-Q2	P-QN3

White has a clear advantage. The black QBP is weak, and if it is exchanged against the white QP then the black QP will be isolated and weak.

White should not be in a hurry. He can slowly strengthen his position. Good moves are : P-N3, P-R3, K-R2, plus some rook moves. A good start would be P-N3, which protects the QRP and makes Q-N2 possible.

17	KR-K1	B-Q2
18	P-K4(?)	

This gives Black counterplay. 18 P-N3 was very good.

| 18 | ... | KR-K1 |
| 19 | K-R1? | |

When we received the first 18 moves in Bristol, where we were making a TV programme, Czech Grandmaster Vlastimil Hort suggested 19 B-B1!, to answer 19...P-QB3 with 20 B-B4. White would still have the advantage.

| 19 | ... | P-QB3 |

Korchnoi now thought for 45 minutes, probably realising that the advantage was gone.

20	P-K5	BPxP
21	BxQP	QR-Q1
22	Q-B4	Q-B1
23	Q-B3?	

Probably overlooking Black's 24th.

| 23 | ... | PxP |
| 24 | BxKP | B-KN5! |

With the safer king and a slight lead in rook mobilisation, Black already has an edge, though there is no reason for White to get into serious difficulties. No reason, that is, except for the clock.

| 25 | QxB | R(Q1)xB |
| 26 | B-B3 | |

Not 26 BxP? RxRch 27 RxR QxB 28 R-K8ch B-B1.

| 26 | ... | R(K1)-Q1 |

And not 26...RxRch 27 RxR BxP? 28 R-K8!

| 27 | K-N2 | B-Q5 |
| 28 | QR-B1 | P-N3 |

A good practical move, creating a flight square for the king, and the possibility 29 Q-B3? R-KB4.

Korchnoi now had less than a minute per move, but after 29 R(K1)-Q1! it is difficult to imagine any result other than a draw.

| 29 | Q-K2? | Q-Q3 |
| 30 | BxB | RxB |

White's next is an oversight. 31 P-N3 R-Q6 32 R-QN1 was necessary and, though it does not look very charming, it would probably still hold.

| 31 | Q-N5?? | R-QN5 |
| 32 | R-K8ch | K-N2 |

33	RxR	QxR
34	Q-K2	

The rook ending after 34 Q-K5ch Q-B3 35 QxQch KxQ 36 R-B2 K-N2 loses against exact play for Black.

34	...	Q-Q4ch
35	P-B3	RxRP
36	R-B2	R-Q5
37	Q-K3	P-QN4
38	P-R4	P-R4
39	Q-K2	P-R5
40	Q-K3	P-N5
41	R-B2	

Instead of playing quickly, as in game 22, Karpov preferred to seal his next move.

Karpov's sealed move was the plausible 41...R-Q6.

Korchnoi said to Keene the same evening that he would resign. But he did not instruct him to notify the arbiters. Next day, when Korchnoi's clock had been running more than half an hour, Michael Stean arrived with a letter of apology.

Resigns

Korchnoi
unlucky 13

GAME TWENTY-EIGHT
30th September and 1st October

Would Karpov try to finish the match quickly? No, at several points he could have chosen sharp continuations but opted for a quiet line; not without justification, for after 27 moves he had a promising endgame, but when adjournment came he was probably lost! In mutual time pressure he had indirectly offered a draw, by repeating moves, but Korchnoi played for a win.

Korchnoi's sealed move may not have been best, but it worked very well because one of Karpov's seconds had told him that the natural defence would lose. The other side had not found a win against it.

So, 5-3. Still rather hopeless for Korchnoi, but, in his 52nd game against Karpov, he was finally able to win with the black pieces!

White: Karpov
Black: Korchnoi

Ruy Lopez

1	P-K4	P-K4
2	N-KB3	N-QB3
3	B-N5	P-QR3
4	B-R4	N-B3
5	0-0	NxP
6	P-Q4	P-QN4
7	B-N3	P-Q4
8	PxP	B-K3
9	P-B3	N-B4

For the first time in the match. Games 8 and 24 gave this annotator the idea that Karpov's answer would be 10 N-Q4, but he chooses a quieter line.

10	B-B2	B-N5
11	R-K1	B-K2
12	QN-Q2	Q-Q2
13	N-N3	N-K3

So far Karpov has used 37 minutes, Korchnoi only 15.

14	P-KR3	B-R4
15	B-B5	N(B3)-Q1
16	B-K3	P-R4

Black has two reasons for postponing castling. First of all, if White plays P-N4, Black may later attack on the K-side with ...P-R4. Secondly, in some variations the white bishop would get to QB5 with gain of time, attacking the black rook.

White's most interesting continuation is 17 P-QR4, but again Karpov plays it safe.

17	B-B5	P-R5
18	BxB	QxB
19	N(N3)-Q2	P-QB3
20	P-QN4	

To make sure that the black pawn majority does not become a steam-roller later.

123

20	...	N-N4
21	Q-K2	P-N3
22	B-N4	BxB
23	PxB	N(Q1)-K3
24	Q-K3	P-R4
25	NxN	QxN
26	QxQ	NxQ

Both pawn majorities are difficult to get moving. 27 P-KB4 N-K3 28 P-B5 N-N4 leads to nothing.

27	PxP	RxP
28	N-B1	

28 P-KB4 N-K3 29 P-N3 was more energetic.

28	...	R-R5
29	QR-Q1	K-K2
30	P-B3	N-K3
31	N-K3	R-Q1
32	N-N4?	

Slight difficulties for White can be seen already, for instance 32 P-R3 P-Q5 33 PxP R(R5)xP with a possible exchange of all rooks and the danger of the black knight getting to ...QB5, but 32 P-N3! was the solution to White's problems.

32	...	N-N4
33	N-K3	N-K3
34	N-N4	N-N2!

Now 35 P-N3 is not possible: 35...R-R6 36 K-N2 R(Q1)-KR1 37 R-KR1 RxR 38 RxR RxR 39 KxR N-B4 40 K-N2 P-Q5 41 PxP NxQP 42 N-K3 K-K3 43 P-B4 P-QB4 44 PxP P-N5!

35	N-K3	N-B4!

After 36 NxNch PxN the white KP would become weak (or he would lose the QRP after 37 R-Q4

R(Q1)-KR1 38 P-KB4 R-R8ch 39 K-B2 RxR 40 KxR R-R8ch).

36	N-B2	R-QB5
37	R-Q3	

37	...	P-Q5!

In spite of time pressure, Black seizes his chance before White strengthens his position with P-R3.

38	P-N4	N-N2
39	NxP	N-K3
40	R(K1)-Q1	NxN
41	PxN	RxNP
42	K-B2	

Karpov wanted to give Korchnoi a difficult choice before adjournment, so he played this move quickly.

Korchnoi now sealed his move.

He thought for half an hour; the choice is between 42...K-K3, 42...R-B5, 42...P-QB4 and 42...R-N7ch. The latter is a difficult decision to make over the board. After 42...R-N7ch 43 R(Q1)-Q2 RxRch 44 RxR K-K3 45 K-K3 or 44...P-QB4 45 R-N2, White seems to hold.

Most players would have sealed the rather neutral 42...K-K3, but out of the envelope came ...

42 ...   P-QB4!?

The natural defence is 43 K-K3 and Keene and Co. were analysing this until 15 minutes before the start of the game. They did not find a win and neither have I. The king and pawn ending is a draw and against 43...P-B5 White plays 44 R(Q3)-Q2, not 44 R-B3? R-N7 45 P-R3 R-N6 46 R-QB1 P-N5! 47 PxP P-R6.

The following moves were played quickly by Karpov; a desperate counter-attack.

43	P-Q5?!	R-N7ch
44	K-N3	RxRP
45	R-K3	P-N5
46	P-K6	R-R6?!

After this White could get drawing chances with 47 RxR. White was threatening P-Q6 ch, but 46...PxP seems good enough for Black. In the game continuation it makes no big difference whether the rook is on ...QR7 or ...QR6.

47	R-K2?	PxP
48	RxPch	K-B2
49	R(Q1)-K1	R-Q2
50	R-N6	R-Q6

Not 50...RxQP 51 R-N7ch.

51	R(K1)-K6	R(Q6)xQP
52	RxKNP	P-R6
53	R(QN6)-KB6ch	K-K2
54	R-K6ch	K-B1
55	R(K6)-KB6ch	K-K2
56	R-K6ch	K-Q1

White has no perpetual check, Black has made the time control and his pawns are ready to run.

57	R-QR6	R-QN2
58	R-N8ch	K-B2
59	R-N7ch	R-Q2
60	R-N5	P-N6
61	RxBPch	

A typical spite check.

| 61 | ... | K-N1 |
| | Resigns | |

GAME TWENTY-NINE
7th and 8th October

Tuesday (October 3rd) the game was postponed by the organizers, because of difficulties with a transformer. Wednesday Korchnoi went to the beach. Thursday the game was postponed at his request because he was suffering from sunburn; he also had a cold. Saturday the game was played, with Korchnoi disappearing between moves, probably to take some medicine.

White: Korchnoi
Black: Karpov

English Opening

1	P-QB4	N-KB3
2	N-QB3	P-K3
3	P-K4	

For the first time in the match.

3	...	P-B4
4	P-K5	N-N1
5	P-Q4	

The pawn sacrifice 5 N-B3 N-QB3 6 P-Q4 has been popular for a couple of years. Timman played it against Karpov in Las Palmas 1977 (and almost lost), Miles played it later the same year in the BBC-TV tournament (and almost won); both games were drawn.

5	...	PxP
6	QxP	N-QB3
7	Q-K4	P-Q3
8	N-B3	PxP
9	NxP	N-B3

Many experts recommend 9...B-Q2.

10	NxN	Q-N3
11	Q-B3	PxN
12	B-K2	B-N2
13	0-0	P-B4
14	Q-R3	

A different plan was Q-K3, P-QN3 and B-N2.

14	...	B-K2
15	B-B3	0-0
16	P-QN3	KR-Q1
17	B-K3	B-B3
18	N-R4	Q-B2
19	BxB	QxB
20	QR-Q1	QR-B1

White probably has a slight edge, but the black position is absolutely defensible.

21	Q-N3	B-Q3
22	Q-R4	B-K2
23	P-B3	K-B1
24	Q-B2	RxR
25	RxR	Q-B2
26	Q-N3	QxQ
27	PxQ	P-KR4
28	K-B2	K-K1
29	K-K2	P-N3
30	N-B3	P-R3

31	N-R4	R-B3
32	R-KR1	B-Q3
33	B-B2	N-Q2

Against very passive play by Black White might get winning chances with B-K1, K-Q3, P-R3 and P-QN4. But Black might have prepared the knight move with ...K-K2.

34	P-KN4!?	PxP
35	R-R8ch	K-K2
36	PxP	

Black's task is easier after 36 B-R4ch P-N4! White's plan is P-N5 and N-B3-K4, but Black does not allow it.

36	...	P-N4
37	B-K3	P-B3
38	N-B3	K-B2
39	R-R7ch	K-K1
40	N-K4	B-K2

Adjourned. Korchnoi sealed his next move, using 36 minutes for it. That left him with just 27 minutes to get to move 56.

41	R-R6	K-B2

Karpov allows Korchnoi to (almost) repeat the position. Why not the active 41...P-R4, trying to prove that it was a serious mistake not to seal 41 R-R8ch or 41 B-Q2?

41...P-R4 42 R-R8ch N-B1 43 B-Q2 R-R3 44 B-B3 K-B2 45 R-R6 K-N2? 46 RxP! BxR 47 BxBch K-N3 48 NxBP gives White good winning chances, but Black can play 45...N-Q2! 46 R-R7ch K-K1 48 R-R8ch K-B2 and hold the game. The idea is very attractive because the black rook becomes active.

However, White has better: 41...P-R4? 42 R-R8ch N-B1 43 K-Q3! and Black is busted: he gets no counterplay on the Q-side, just a new weakness, so Korchnoi's sealed move was not so bad after all.

42	R-R7ch	K-B1
43	R-R8ch	

Again it is difficult to argue against many hours of analysis by a whole team, but I analysed B-Q2 (on move 41!) and found very good winning chances.

43	...	K-B2
44	B-Q2	N-B1

Probably the best defence. 44...N-K4 45 N-B2 R-Q3? would be a bad idea because of 46 B-B3 N-B3 47 N-K4 N-Q5ch 48 K-Q3 R-Q2 49 NxQBP.

45	R-R1	K-N3
46	R-Q1	P-B4(?)

Passive defence is not attractive, but how could White break through? The text-move would have been better ..... on move 36!

47	N-B2	B-Q3
48	B-B3	N-Q2
49	PxPch	PxP

50 P-KN4!   N-N3

A very ugly move; Black prevents R-Q5 but the knight will be misplaced during the rest of the game.

The position was already difficult; 50...N-K4? 51 RxBch, 50...N-B3 51 BxN KxB 52 R-Q5 and 50...PxP? 51 N-K4 were some of the ways to lose quickly.

51 K-B3

51 B-R5 may be even stronger. Needless to say Korchnoi was in time pressure.

51	...	B-K2
52	B-R5	R-B3
53	K-N2	PxP

Karpov thought for 15 minutes here and then played the next moves quickly. Korchnoi still had a couple of minutes left to get to the next time control at move 56.

54	NxP	R-K3
55	K-B3	B-B3
56	NxB	

The exchange of knight for bishop is not very desirable for White in this position; the black bishop being hemmed in by two of the black pawns, but White does not want to permit ...B-Q5 and keeps good winning chances because of the bad position of the black knight.

56	...	RxNch
57	K-N4!	N-B1

58 B-Q8!   R-B5ch

58...R-Q3 59 RxR NxR 60 BxP is a win for White because the black king is badly placed, for instance 60...K-B2 61 B-K3 N-N2 62 K-B5.

59 K-N3   R-B4

59...R-Q5 60 RxR PxR 61 K-N4 N-Q3 62 BxP N-K5 63 B-B4 is tricky enough, but a draw for Black is not to be seen.

60	P-R4	K-B2
61	R-Q3	R-K4

Korchnoi was in time pressure again: 11 minutes for 11 moves.

62 K-N4   K-N3

Giving up the idea of sacrificing the NP. After 62...K-K3 63 BxP it is still not possible for Black to get his knight into play or his king to the defence of the queen-side, for instance 63...N-K2 64 B-B4.

63	P-R5	R-K5ch
64	K-B3	R-B5ch

After 64...R-K4 65 R-Q7 the threat of R-QB7 would be very strong.

Another try is 64...K-B4 65 BxP N-R2 66 B-Q2 N-B3 67 B-B3 N-Q5ch 68 BxN PxB 69 P-N4 R-R5 - but White wins immediately with 66 R-Q7!

65	K-K3	R-R5
66	R-Q5	

Now it is clear that White is winning.

66	...	R-R6ch
67	K-Q2!	

After 67 K-K4 the black knight would get into play with check.

67	...	RxP
68	RxBP	R-N1

68...N-Q3? 69 R-B6.

69	R-B6ch	K-B4
70	RxP	P-N5
71	R-KB6ch	K-K5
72	B-B7!	

Last move before the time control and a mating threat!

72	...	R-N7ch
73	K-B3	R-N2
74	B-R2	

Just for fun.

74	...	R-KR2
75	B-N8	R-QN2
76	B-N3	R-N8
77	R-B4ch!	K-K6
78	R-B8	N-K2
79	P-R6	Resigns

Because of 79...N-B3 80 P-R7 NxP 81 B-B2ch.

Good endgame play by Korchnoi, but it is not easy to say where Karpov made the decisive mistake; maybe on move 46?

5-4!! From a hopeless position, Korchnoi came back into the match. It must have been difficult for Karpov to adjust to the new situation. The last time he lost two successive games was in his "secret" training match against the same opponent in 1971. The only other known occasion in his whole chess career was as far back as 1967 when young Anatoly lost the two last rounds in the semi-final of the Soviet Junior Championship, the lucky winners being Levon Grigorian and Alexander Bokuchava.

GAME THIRTY
10th October

Many experts predicted that Karpov would take time out. He didn't, but he played the English Opening for the third time in the match; maybe he wanted a peaceful draw? Wrong again: he played for a win and declined a draw offer at move 34.

White: Karpov
Black: Korchnoi

English Opening

1	P-QB4	N-KB3
2	N-QB3	P-Q4
3	PxP	NxP
4	P-KN3	P-KN3
5	B-N2	NxN
6	NPxN	B-N2
7	N-B3	0-0
8	0-0	P-QB4

Many masters prefer White in this type of position because he has more centre pawns, but Korchnoi doesn't mind playing Black.

9	R-N1	N-B3
10	Q-R4	N-R4
11	P-Q3	P-N3

11...BxP 12 B-R6 gives White a strong initiative and Black cannot keep the pawn.

12	Q-R4	B-N2
13	B-R6	BxB

Together with the following move, a good practical solution, but White maintains a slight advantage.

14	QxB	BxN
15	BxB	R-B1
16	B-N2	Q-Q2
17	QR-K1	P-QN4

18	R-N1

Was this Karpov's plan when he played the previous move? Probably not, but the move in itself is not bad; it is not clear that White could gain anything on the king-side.

18	...	R-N1
19	Q-K3	Q-Q3
20	KR-Q1	P-QR3
21	R-Q2	KR-B1
22	R(Q2)-N2	N-B3
23	Q-Q2	

The plan is P-QR4, but here it was bad because of the reply ...P-N5.

23	...	N-K4
24	Q-B4	N-Q2
25	QxQ	PxQ
26	B-R3	R-Q1
27	P-R4	PxP
28	BxN	RxR

29	RxR	RxB
30	R-R2	

A critical line is 30 R-N8ch K-N2 31 R-QR8 R-N2 32 RxP R-N6 33 P-QB4 P-R6 34 K-N2 R-N7, without winning chances for White.

30	...	K-B1
31	RxP	R-R2
32	K-B1	K-K2
33	K-K1	K-Q2
34	K-Q2	P-KR4

It was here that Korchnoi offered a draw. White has a very slight advantage because his pawns are "one island" against Black's three, but as a wise man once said: "all rook endings are drawn".

35	K-B2	R-R1
36	R-QB4	K-K3
37	P-R4	R-QN1
38	R-K4ch	K-Q2
39	R-R4	R-QR1
40	R-KB4	K-K3
41	R-B4	R-R2

Karpov sealed his next move (42 R-K4ch). Next day a draw offer from the Russian camp arrived.

The draw offer came less than two hours before the game was to be resumed. Korchnoi was asleep, but his aides woke him up, after which the draw was agreed very quickly. The result was celebrated almost as a victory in Korchnoi's camp.

FIDE President Euwe made his reservation for the flight Amsterdam-Manila when he saw the adjourned position of game 20. He cancelled it again when he saw the result of that game. Ten days later he did go to Baguio, ready to crown the champion. After game 31 he gave up waiting for a result and left!

In Korchnoi's camp it was seen as a conspiracy between Campomanes and the Russians that the Ananda Marga question was resurrected immediately after Euwe's departure. However, it is worth remembering that it was Korchnoi who brought up the question of personal security before the start of the match and that Campomanes immediately answered that the players' personal safety was guaranteed by the Philippine authorities. It may be added that words like "attempted murder" and "security risk" have a very real meaning for Campomanes; in October 1975 his friend, and adviser to President Marcos, de Vega, who had done a lot for Philippine chess, was shot down in his office.

White tries to open the queen-side but must abandon the idea. He tries in the centre, but cannot advance. He looks at the king-side … and on the first move after the time control he tries the central breakthrough! At adjournment it is exactly the same material as in the previous game: rook and six pawns versus rook and six pawns.

White: Korchnoi
Black: Karpov

Queen's Gambit Declined

1	P-QB4	P-K3
2	N-QB3	P-Q4
3	P-Q4	N-KB3
4	PxP	PxP
5	B-N5	B-K2
6	P-K3	0-0
7	B-Q3	QN-Q2
8	N-B3	R-K1
9	Q-B2	P-B3
10	0-0	N-B1
11	BxN	BxB
12	P-QN4	B-N5
13	N-Q2	R-B1
14	B-B5	BxB
15	QxB	Q-Q2

A known improvement on Reshevsky-Miagmarsuren, Sousse 1967, but Korchnoi goes into the endgame with great pleasure.

16	QxQ	NxQ
17	P-QR4	B-K2
18	KR-N1	N-B3

19 P-R5

White has gained the QB5 square, but where is he going to break through?

19	...	P-QR3
20	N-R4	B-B1
21	N-B5	R-K2
22	K-B1	N-K1
23	K-K2	N-Q3
24	K-Q3	R(B1)-K1
25	R-K1	P-KN3
26	R-K2	P-B3
27	QR-K1	B-R3
28	N(Q2)-N3	B-B1
29	N-Q2	B-R3
30	P-R3	K-B2
31	P-N4	B-B1
32	P-B3	R-Q1
33	N(Q2)-N3	N-N4
34	R-KB1	B-R3

35 P-B4

It looks as if White gives up the idea of P-K4.

35	...	B-B1
36	N-Q2	N-Q3
37	R(B1)-K1	P-R3
38	R-KB1	R-N1
39	R-QR1	R(N1)-K1
40	R(QR1)-K1	R-N1

40...R-Q1 was better if Black wanted to avoid White's P-K4, but it looks as if Karpov wanted to provoke it.

It is rather astonishing that Karpov spent less than 10 minutes on moves 31-40; he still had more than an hour left on his clock at move 40!

41 P-K4!?

Looks risky, but Korchnoi may have thought that after the adjournment he would't get a chance to play this move.

41	...	PxPch
42	N(Q2)xP	N-N4

Black may have hoped that White would over-reach himself with 43 P-B5? PxP 44 PxP R-Q1 45 N-K6 R-Q4 (even 45...RxPch 46 NxR R-Q2 is good for Black!).

43	N-B3	RxR
44	RxR	BxN
45	NPxB	R-Q1

45...NxN 46 KxN R-K1 47 RxR KxR 48 P-Q5 PxP 49 K-Q4 P-KN4! is a clear draw, but 47 R-QN2! R-K2 48 P-Q5 PxP 49 K-Q4 is difficult for Black.

46	NxN	RPxN
47	P-B5	

Adjourned. The black position looks solid, but closer study reveals some dangers: White has more space and the breaks P-R6 and P-Q5 can become dangerous against careless defence. There is a problem about what to do with the black king: on Q2 it protects the white QP!

47 ... PxP

Generally expected and almost forced. 47...P-N4 just leaves the advanced white KBP well protected.

The alternative is 47...R-QR1 with the idea 48 R-QR2 P-R4! This gives Black sufficient counterplay but (47...R-QR1) 48 PxPch KxP 49 R-K7 is a different story, for example 49...RxP 50 RxP R-R6ch 51 K-K4 RxP 52 N-N6.

48 PxP R-KN1

After 48...R-QR1 49 R-QR2 K-K2 50 K-B3 P-R4 51 P-R4, Black would be in a curious zugzwang. White is not threatening K-N4 because of the reply ...R-Q1, but after 51...K-Q2 52 K-N4! K-B2 53 P-Q5 he gets some winning chances; still it is difficult to find a clear win and I stubbornly stick to my opinion, from an article written directly after adjournment: this was Black's best defence and it probably draws.

An interesting ethical problem: how much to write about an adjourned game? The article could be read in Copenhagen and Stockholm before the game was resumed.

49 K-B3

The best move or psychology? I analysed 49 R-QR2, thinking Black had to answer 49...R-QR1 with the same problems as in the previous note.

49 ...   R-K1?

Definitely wrong; after White's next move he gets the maximum effect from his king and his rook in connection with the two breaks P-R6 and P-Q5.

49...R-N4 is very complicated, but there is no win for White after 50 R-K6 RxP 51 P-R6 PxP 52 RxQBP P-QR4 53 R-N6 R-B6ch 54 K-Q2 P-N5 55 P-B6 K-K2! (not 55...K-K3? 56 P-B7ch K-Q2 57 R-B6 K-B1 58 P-Q5 and wins).

Even 49...R-N8 is interesting: after 50 P-R6 PxP 51 R-K6 P-QR4 52 RxQBP R-N6ch 53 K-Q2 P-R5 54 R-R6 P-R6 55 P-Q5 P-N5 56 P-Q6? P-R7! Black draws but 56 P-B6! K-K2 57 P-B7! wins.

And what about 49...R-N6ch; is

White bluffing? 50 K-N4 R-Q6 51 P-R6 RxQPch 52 K-R5 PxP 53 K-N6 P-N5 leads to a draw and 51 R-K4 R-Q8! 52 P-R6 PxP 53 K-R5 R-QR8ch 54 K-N6 P-N5 leads to the same result.

This ending will be analysed for years.

50 R-Q2!   R-K5

50...R-K8 looks better at first sight, but after 51 P-Q5 R-QB8ch 51 K-N2! RxP 53 PxP RxQBP 54 R-Q7ch, or 53...PxP 54 P-R6 White wins. My guess is that Karpov overlooked 52 K-N2! (52 R-QB2 R-QR8 leads to a draw).

51	K-N4	K-K1
52	P-R6	PxP
53	K-R5	K-Q2
54	K-N6	

54 KxRP?? K-B2 wins for Black!

K-N7, followed by P-Q5, is now a murderous threat.

54 ...   P-N5

So that 55 K-N7? P-N6 56 P-Q5 R-QN5ch.

55 P-Q5   PxP

56	RxPch	K-B1
57	R-Q3!	

Stops the QNP and prepares the decisive entry via the KN-file; Black is lost.

57	...	P-QR4
58	R-KN3	P-N6

Or 58...P-R5 59 P-B6 R-K1 60 R-N4.

59	K-B6!	K-N1
60	RxPch	K-R2
61	R-N7ch	K-R3
62	R-N6ch	K-R2
63	K-N5	P-R5
64	RxP	R-KB5
65	RxP	P-R6
66	R-R6ch	K-N1
67	RxP	RxP
68	R-KN3	R-B3
69	R-N8ch	K-B2
70	R-N7ch	K-B1
71	R-KR7	Resigns

5-5!!! Incredible. For the first time in his career, Karpov has only made half a point in four games: he must be shaken.

Soviet Sports Minister Ivonin arrived in Baguio just in time to see his hero resign.

Reports from Baguio note that Karpov has lost weight, but this is quite normal for a participant in a world championship match.

"This game was 80% drawn", said Keene, "they don't know how to analyse."

How did Korchnoi win game 31? Oh no problem, his lucky number is 13: he arrived with 13 suitcases, desiring to be World Champion number 13, he set up his headquarters in a villa with 13 rooms and he won a game on the 13th of September; game 31, on a 13th, couldn't go wrong!

There were reports that there were fantastic victory celebrations in Korchnoi's camp when it was 4-5, but when it was 5-5 he was very quiet and just said: "The next game decides - it's like a lottery."

GAME THIRTY-TWO
17th and 18th October

Karpov looks tired, he looks serious, is he a beaten man? Korchnoi wears the same suit as last week; can he win only in those clothes?

The journalists want something to happen, and what about the rumour that the match has to be suspended for a month to enable the players and their seconds to play in the Chess Olympiad in Buenos Aires? They cannot do that, certainly not at 5-5! Well, you never know with FIDE and wars between the Greek states were suspended for the duration of the Olympic Games...

Another problem has flared up again: it is rumoured that Karpov threatened to withdraw from the match if the Ananda Marga gurus were not sent away from Baguio. Philippine authorities agree that the two who have been convicted of attempted murder must be considered a security risk. A long meeting was held and in the morning of this Tuesday Keene had to go to the police station to sign a statement guaranteeing that these people had left Baguio City. The Russian delegation connects this problem with the Zoukhar dispute; they say that the parapsychologist is no longer bound by the gentleman's agreement because the Korchnoi group has broken its part of the agreement.

All this is very difficult for outsiders to follow. Who is right? Probably nobody. During the game Zoukhar conquers a seat in the fourth row. Miraculously, Korchnoi did not notice this move.

On Saturday Karpov saw the Soviet basketball team lose its world championship to Yugoslavia in Manila, by one point after extra time. Somebody thinks this must have demoralised him, but is he really interested in basketball?

The game begins. It is a Pirc but suddenly it is an old-fashioned Benoni. Probably Karpov likes the white position and Korchnoi doesn't mind the black one, but he gets into time pressure! Karpov has good chances on the king-side... Suddenly he grabs a pawn on the queen-side...

You know the rest, Karpov wins 6-5 - it's all over.

White: Karpov
Black: Korchnoi

Pirc/Benoni Defence

1	P-K4	P-Q3
2	P-Q4	N-KB3
3	N-QB3	P-KN3

Of the not very good defences Korchnoi turned to when he gave up the Spanish duel, the Pirc was the least bad!

4	N-B3	B-N2
5	B-K2	0-0
6	0-0	P-B4

Not recommended in the books. In the *Encyclopaedia of Chess Openings* a game is given with the continuation 7 PxP PxP 8 QxQ RxQ 9 B-K3 P-N3 10 KR-Q1 B-Q2 11 N-K5 N-K1, which does not look satisfactory for Black. A possible improvement is 10...N-B3, but White must keep some advantage.

Karpov decides not to exchange queens. It looks like a psychological victory for Korchnoi.

7 P-Q5   N-R3

A standard position in the Benoni (1 P-Q4 P-QB4 2 P-Q5), often played by Lothar Schmid! It can also arise from a Sicilian: 1 P-K4 P-QB4 2 N-KB3 P-KN3 3 P-Q4 B-N2 4 P-Q5, but among leading Grandmasters it has been played very little since Leonid Stein's premature death.

8 B-KB4   N-B2
9 P-QR4   P-N3

A flexible set-up. 9...P-QR3 is also possible.

10 R-K1   B-N2

The idea is to put pressure on the white QP so that he cannot advance his KP. After due preparation, Black will play either ...P-QN4 or ...P-K3.

11 B-B4   N-R4?!

Very dubious. 11...P-QR3 looks normal.

12 B-KN5   N-B3

13 Q-Q3   P-QR3
14 QR-Q1   R-N1
15 P-R3

The interesting thing about Karpov's treatment of the opening is that he did not play this move early; after Black's loss of time he permits himself this luxury.

15 ...   N-Q2
16 Q-K3   B-QR1
17 B-R6   P-QN4

Karpov has spent 75 minutes, Korchnoi 105!

18 BxB   KxB
19 B-B1   N-B3
20 PxP   PxP
21 N-K2   B-N2
22 N-N3   R-QR1
23 P-B3   R-R5
24 B-Q3   Q-R1?!

Very risky, taking the queen away from the defence of the dark squares on the king-side. Already his previous move was probably the result of an under-estimation of the danger.

Karpov had an hour for the next 16 moves - meaning that he was not playing this game at his usual speed!

But Korchnoi had only 18 minutes left.

25	P-K5!	PxP

The refutation of 25...N(B3)xP is 26 N-R5ch PxN 27 Q-N5ch K-R1 28 Q-R6 P-B4 29 PxBPe.p. NxKBP 30 RxP.

26	QxKP	NxP
27	BxQNP	R-R2
28	N-R4	

Maybe best, and certainly it is a very practical move: the many sacrificial threats are difficult to meet for a player who has spent too much time on some subtle detail in the opening.

28	...	B-B1
29	B-K2	B-K3
30	P-QB4	

Black comes just too late; he was threatening ...Q-N1, with an excellent position!

30	...	N-N5
31	QxP	Q-N1?

31...N-B7 was a better try.

32	B-B1	R-B1
33	Q-KN5	K-R1
34	R-Q2	N-B3

Against 34...BxBP 35 BxB RxB White had 36 RxP!
Karpov has consolidated a good position with a pawn more, but there are still some technical difficulties. However, Korchnoi has only two minutes for six moves...

35	Q-R6	R-N1
36	N-B3	Q-KB1
37	Q-K3	K-N2?

37...R-QN2 is much better.

38	N-N5	B-Q2

39	P-N4!	

Decisive. This is the move Black must never allow.

39	...	Q-R1
40	P-N5	N-QR4
41	P-N6	

Adjourned. Korchnoi sealed his move.

The sealed move was 41...R-N2. Next day at noon Korchnoi resigned the game and the match.

There were some pretty good guesses about the length of the match (in duration it is the longest title match ever - just over three months, but it took Alekhine 34 games to beat Capablanca in 1927). It has been said that Korchnoi only expected thirty games when he thought about how much caviar to take to Baguio. Not a bad guess, but Mrs Annette Keene hit the final date exactly when she decided to go to the Philippines at half-time; nobody could have known when the match was half-way through, not even Korchnoi's seconds, but she left for Baguio on Saturday September 2; they call that female intuition.

The B.B.C. decided to have the last weekly *World Chess Championship Report* on the 23rd of October, not because they guessed when the match was going to end, but simply because three months is enough!

Korchnoi's Open Letter

To
L. I. Brezhnev
General Secretary of the Communist Party
President of the Supreme Soviet of the USSR
Marshall of the USSR

V. L. Korchnoi
Int. Chess Grandmaster
Challenger for the World
Chess Championship
Resident in Switzerland

Open Letter

Dear Mr. Brezhnev,

As a professional chess grandmaster, recently a citizen of the USSR, now resident in Switzerland, I turn to you.

Two years ago I emigrated to the West, since it was no longer in my power to bear the extreme and hostile attitude of Party, Soviet and Sport leaders, since I no longer had the possibility to continue my creative activity in the Soviet Union.

My family remained in the Soviet Union, my wife and son. In spite of the fact that they are loyal Soviet citizens they submitted a request in July, 1977 to emigrate from the Soviet Union. They did this, impelled by their love for a husband and a father. November, 1977 this request was refused. In private conversation Soviet police chiefs left no doubt open that the members of my family are hostages, human beings who have chosen to suffer penance for my escape.

About one year has passed since their request for emigration. The situation of my family is now catastrophic. They have been robbed of the means of their existence and of the possibility of working or studying. The authorities confront them with suspicion and hatred, ordinary people avoid all contact with them. For my family there has now been a severe dimunition of all the rights guaranteed by the Constitution - but there has been no reduction in their duties! My son, who already a year ago declared his intention of leaving his homeland, has nevertheless been obstinately called up for military service.

You, Marshall of the Soviet Union, praise the heroism of a Muhammed Ali, who refused to fight in Vietnam. My son also does not want to fight. He does not want to be a soldier of the state which has unscrupulously degraded his father.

KORCHNOI'S OPEN LETTER

Is it not curious, my dear Chairman of the Supreme Soviet, that the guilty go free while it is those who are without protection who are punished, punished for their own incapacity to work, for the appearance of unhealthy sporting relations, and finally for the professional incompetence of the Soviet leaders. The practice of punishing political hostages has, unfortunately, been common throughout the entire world, but how, my dear President, does that suit the complexion of one of the regimes which significantly helps to determine world political fashions?!

In these days a Match is beginning in the Philippines for the World Chess Championship between myself and the Soviet Grandmaster and World Champion Anatoly Karpov.

Soviet leaders have declared more than once that sport must be separated from politics. It is self-evident that those states should also adhere to this principle who will participate in the World Sport Olympiad destined for Moscow in 1980.

I appeal to your political common sense, my dear General Secretary: In order to ensure that this match for the World Chess Championship should take place under normal conditions, without political complications, I beg you to allow my family to depart from the Soviet Union.

I appeal to you to demonstrate the goodwill necessary for the fulfillment of the conditions of the Helsinki International Agreement, which prescribes the reunification of divided families.

I invoke your mercy, Mr. Chairman; I beg you to show compassion for two citizens of the USSR, whose life, by decree of fate, is no longer bound to the life of Soviet society. Permit them to leave the Soviet Union.

Chess Grandmaster

Viktor Korchnoi

1-7-1978

cc: Soviet Ambassador in Manila

EPILOGUE

Games are not won, they are lost! I heard several experts saying this half-way through the match and there is a lot of truth in it, but on many occasions you might just as well have said that the won games in this match were not won. Towards the end, Karpov's trouble was that the drawn games were not drawn.

The match is over. Let us relax and play with words. And let us mention Robert Byrne, the prophet. He predicted 6-5, just as he had forseen the exact outcome of the Spassky-Fischer match (12½-8½). If in the future it becomes impossible to play world championship matches, just ask Byrne who should be champion.

There were lots of good predictions. Most experts foretold a victory for Karpov. I am quite proud of my own judgement: "they are of almost equal strength, but a diabolical invention will cost Korchnoi the match, it is called the chess clock." And certainly Michael Stean was proven right on various counts: Korchnoi had a plus in the endgame and it looks as if the older player had more stamina. Karpov can probably be said to have had a slight plus in the opening, though Korchnoi had considerable success with some prepared lines at the beginning of the match.

Many of Korchnoi's deep moves certainly cost too much time, so too did many moves which were not of any special difficulty. All this was predictable. It was also expected that Karpov would play more quickly, but in some games he took this to such an extent thet there can be no other explanation than the nervous tension. Well maybe there is another possible reason/explanation, but if there is we have yet to hear of it.

Karpov refused to reveal his tactics before the match - very natural. He said he would explain many things after the match. It is perfectly possible that he will explain that he planned to play quickly in some games because he might want to push Korchnoi into a second time scramble! If you have spent less than 90 minutes for the first 40 moves and reached a bad position, you have to continue quickly and make it impossible for your opponent to adjourn before the second time control at move 56.

Several comments can be made. Firstly, it didn't quite work. Secondly, Korchnoi, on several occasions, spent so much time on his sealed move that he got into time pressure the next day. Thirdly, the idea is insane when the player who is moving quickly has a won game!! In game 22 Karpov played much too quickly after move 40 and allowed Korchnoi to save a hopeless position. And in game 31 Karpov would never have found himself in difficulties if he had not played blitz.

So any trainer or second must give both players bad marks for their handling of the clock, but of course this question is closely related to nerves.

What about the seconds? Korchnoi's may feel some guilt for Black's 42nd move in game 5. To lose the "Unloseable" game 13 was probably his own doing.

Karpov's seconds must have made some mistakes in the last three games he lost. According to some reports, Karpov was so tired that he did not take as much part in the analysis as he ought to have done. In general both teams probably worked quite well, but we know less about the Russians than about the Korchnoi camp, for instance Keene has stated publicly that 10...P-KN3 in game 8 was not part of any team preparation.

Where did Karpov really have a plus apart from not getting into time trouble very often? It may be argued that he was more objective and that he played best in quiet middle-game positions where nothing much was the matter, but we probably end up at the chess clock again and at the word "practical". Karpov is practical and he plays good moves quickly in positions where Korchnoi looks for deep moves and combinations which are probably not there at all.

I have read that the level of play was much lower than in Spassky-Fischer 1972. This is difficult to discuss because all title matches are disappointing! Too many nerves. In my opinion it was difficult to equal the worst Reykjavik games and the Baguio match never reached that level! But in Reykjavik there were some wonderful games by Fischer which the public remembers; these games were, in part, the result of Spassky playing nowhere near his best. The match in Baguio was more balanced, but long, tough endgames do not apeal to the public at large.

As has been said many times, the match was too long and FIDE will probably change the rules. It was too long not only for the players, but for a lot of other people too; for instance for all those who wrote about it. That it rained too much in Baguio was a common complaint in news releases.

I congratulate the winner. I congratulate the loser, who fought with a fantastic never-say-die spirit; he came incredibly close to winning the title, but there can be only one winner, only one champion.

This book was written in Spain, Holland, England and Denmark. Originally I had decided not to write any book about this match of unlimited duration, but Kevin O'Connell and David Levy of The Philidor Press changed my mind (we are still friends!). They provided some of the background material and corrected language mistakes. They also found a typesetter who was willing to work even on Sundays if necessary. There will be many books on this match, but this was to be the first one. The book went to press before Korchnoi's resignation was officially announced!!!